JEREMY TAYLOR

ΧΡΙΣΙΣ ΤΕΛΕΙΩΤΙΚΗ
Perfective Unction:
A Discourse of Confirmation

SEMINARY STREET PRESS
The Library of Anglican Theology
Number 1

Published by Seminary Street Press, the Library of Anglican Theology seeks to provide newly typeset editions of important works from the Anglican tradition for a wide array of contemporary readers—Christian laypeople, historians of the Church, seminary students, bishops, priests, deacons, catechists, and theologians. The Library will provide a rich foundation on which to build as Anglicans continue to theologically engage with the pressing questions of our time.

Series Editor
CHRISTOPHER POORE

Jeremy Taylor

*Perfective Unction:
A Discourse of Confirmation*

Editor
Reginald Heber

Revised and Corrected
Charles Page Eden

SEMINARY STREET PRESS
GALESBURG, ILLINOIS

Galesburg, Illinois

2021 Paperback Edition
ISBN: 979-8-70-944740-0

facebook.com/SeminaryStreetPress
Twitter: @SeminaryStPress
Instagram: @SeminaryStreetPress
seminarystreetpress@gmail.com

All rights reserved.
While the work itself is in the public domain,
no part of this newly typeset edition may be reproduced or transmitted
in any form or by any means, electronic or mechanical,
without the publisher's permission in writing.

Contents

Epistle Dedicatory 1

Introduction 9

§1. Of the divine original, warranty, and institution of the holy rite of confirmation. 14

§2. The rite of confirmation is a perpetual and never ceasing ministry. 35

§3. The holy rite of imposition of hands for the giving the Holy Spirit, or confirmation, was actually continued and practised by all the succeeding ages of the purest and primitive church . . . 42

§4. The bishops were always and the only ministers of confirmation. 51

§5. The whole procedure or ritual of confirmation is by prayer and imposition of hands. 61

§6. Many great graces and blessings are consequent to the worthy reception and due ministry of confirmation. 66

§7. Of preparation to confirmation and the circumstances of receiving it. 77

Εἰ Πνεῦμα ἅγιον ἐλάβετε πιστεύσαντες
Have ye received the Holy Ghost since ye believed?

ACTS 19:2

Epistle Dedicatory

To His Grace James Duke of Ormond,
 Lord Lieutenant General, and General Governor of His Majesty's Kingdom of Ireland, One of the Lords of His Majesty's Most Honourable Privy Council of His Majesty's Kingdoms of England, Scotland, and Ireland, &c. and Knight of the Most Noble Order of the Garter.

May it please your grace,

It is not any confidence that I have dexterously performed this charge that gives me the boldness to present it to your grace. I have done it as well as I could, and for the rest my obedience will bear me out: for I took not this task upon myself, but was entreated to it by them who have power to command me. But yet it is very necessary that it should be addressed to your grace, who are, as Sozomen[1] said of Theodosius, *certaminum magister, et orationum judex constitutus*: you are appointed the great master of our arguings, and are most fit to be the judge of our discourses, especially when they do relate and pretend to public influence and advantages to the church. We all are witnesses of your zeal to promote true religion, and every day find you to be a great patron to this very poor church, which groans under the calamities and permanent effects of a war acted by intervals for above four hundred years; such which the intermedial sun-shines of peace could

---

[1] [In orat. ad Theod. p. 4 init.]

but very weakly repair. Our churches are still demolished, much of the revenues irrecoverably swallowed by sacrilege and digested by an unavoidable impunity; religion infinitely divided and parted into formidable sects; the people extremely ignorant and wilful by inheritance; superstitiously irreligious and uncapable of reproof. And amidst these and very many more inconveniences, it was greatly necessary that God should send us such a king, and he send us such a viceroy, who weds the interests of religion and joins them to his heart.

For we do not look upon your grace only as a favourer of the church's temporal interest, though even for that the souls of the relieved clergy do daily bless you; neither are you our patron only as the Cretans were to Homer or the Aleuadæ to Simonides, Philip to Theopompus or Severus to Oppianus; but as Constantine and Theodosius were to Christians; that is, desirous that true religion should be promoted, that the interest of souls should be advanced, that truth should flourish and wise principles should be entertained, as the best cure against those evils which this nation hath too often brought upon themselves. In order to which excellent purposes it is hoped that the reduction of the holy rite of confirmation into use and holy practice may contribute some very great moments. For besides that the great usefulness of this ministry will greatly endear the episcopal order, to which (that I may use S. Hierome's[2] words) "if there be not attributed a more than common power and authority, there will be as many schisms as priests;" it will also be a means of endearing the persons of the prelates to their flocks, when the people shall be convinced that there is, or may be if they please, a perpetual entercourse of blessings and love between them; when God by their holy hands refuses not to give to the people the earnest of an eternal inheritance, when by them He blesses; and that "the grace of our Lord Jesus, and the love of God, and the communication of His spirit," is conveyed to all persons capable of the grace, by the conduct and on the hands and prayers of their bishops.

---

[2] [tom. iv. part. 2. col. 295.]

And indeed not only very many single persons, but even the whole church of Ireland hath need of confirmation. We have most of us contended for false religions and unchristian propositions; and now that by God's mercy and the prosperity and piety of his sacred majesty the church is broken from her cloud, and many are reduced to the true religion and righteous worship of God, we cannot but call to mind how the holy fathers of the primitive church often have declared themselves in councils, and by a perpetual discipline, that such persons who are returned from sects and heresies into the bosom of the church should not be rebaptized, but that the bishops should impose hands on them in confirmation. It is true that this was designed to supply the defect of those schismatical conventicles who did not use this holy rite; for this rite of confirmation hath had the fate to be opposed only by the schismatical and puritan parties of old, the Novatians or Cathari, and the Donatists; and of late by the Jesuits and new Cathari, the puritans and presbyterians; the same evil spirit of contradiction keeping its course in the same channel and descending regularly amongst men of the same principles. But therefore in the restitution of a man, or company of men, or a church, the holy primitives in the council of C.P., Laodicea, and Orange, thought that to confirm such persons was the most agreeable discipline, not only because such persons did not in their little and dark assemblies use this rite, but because they always greatly wanted it. For it is a sure rule in our religion and is of an eternal truth, that 'they who keep not the unity of the church have not the Spirit of God;' and therefore it is most fit should receive the ministry of the Spirit when they return to the bosom of the church, that so indeed they may keep the unity of the spirit in the bond of peace. And therefore Asterius[3] bishop of Amasia compares confirmation to the ring with which the father of the prodigal adorned his returning son; *Datur nempe prodigo post stolam et annulus, nempe symbolum intelligibilis signaculi Spiritus.* And as the Spirit of God, the holy Dove, extended His mighty wings over the creation, and hatched the new-born world from its seminal powers to light and operation and life and motion;

---

[3] [Apud Photium, biblioth. cod. 271. p. 502., 5.]

so in the regeneration of the souls of men He gives a new being, and heat and life, procedure and perfection, wisdom and strength: and because that this was ministered by the bishop's hands in confirmation, was so firmly believed by all the primitive church, therefore it became a law and an universal practice in all those ages in which men desired to be saved by all means. The Latin church and the Greek always did use it, and the blessings of it, which they believed consequent to it, they expressed in a holy prayer which in the Greek Euchologion[4] they have very anciently and constantly used, "Thou, O Lord, the most compassionate and great King of all, graciously impart to this person the seal of the gift of Thy holy, almighty, and adorable Spirit." For, as an ancient Greek said truly and wisely,[5] "the Father is reconciled, and the Son is the reconciler; but to them who are by baptism and repentance made friends of God, the Holy Spirit is collated as a gift." They well knew what they received in this ministration, and therefore wisely laid hold of it and would not let it go.

This was anciently ministered by apostles, and ever after by the bishops, and religiously received by kings and greatest princes; and I have read that S. Sylvester confirmed Constantine the emperor: and when they made their children servants of the holy Jesus and soldiers under His banner and bonds-men of His institution, then they sent them to the bishop to be confirmed; who did it sometimes by such ceremonies that the solemnity of the ministry might with greatest religion addict them to the service of their great Lord. We read in Adrevaldus[6] that Charles Martel entering into a league with bishop Liutprandus sent his son Pepin to him, *ut more christianorum fidelium ejus capillum primus attonderet ac pater illi spiritualis existeret*, that he might after the manner of Christians first cut his hair (in token of service to Christ) and (in confirming him) he should be his spiritual father. And

---

[4] [Goar., p. 355.] Αὐτὸς δέσποτα, παμβασιλεῦ, εὔσπλαγχνε, χαρίσαι αὐτῷ καὶ τὴν σφραγῖδα τῆς δωρεᾶς τοῦ ἁγίου καὶ παντοδυνάμου καὶ προσκυνητοῦ σου Πνεύματος.
[5] Ὁ μὲν Πατὴρ διήλλακται, ὁ δὲ Υἱὸς διήλλαξε, τὸ δὲ Πνεῦμα τὸ ἅγιον φίλοις ἤδη καταστᾶσι δῶρον.
[6] De miraculis S. Benedict., lib. i. c. 14. [apud. Joann. a Bosco, biblioth. Floriac., p. 31. 8vo. Lugd. 1605.]

something like this we find concerning William earl of Warren and Surrey,[7] who when he had dedicated the church of S. Pancratius and the priory of Lewes, received confirmation and gave seisure *per capillos capitis mei* (says he in the charter) *et fratris mei Radulphi de Warrena, quos abscidit cum cultello de capitibus nostris Henricus episcopus Wintoniensis*; 'by the hairs of my head and of my brother's, which Henry bishop of Winchester cut off before the altar:' meaning (according to the ancient custom) in confirmation, when they by that solemnity addicted themselves to the free servitude of the Lord Jesus. The ceremony is obsolete and changed, but the mystery can never. And indeed that is one of the advantages in which we can rejoice concerning the ministration of this rite in the church of England and Ireland, that whereas it was sometimes clouded, sometimes hindered, and sometimes hurt, by the appendage of needless and useless ceremonies, it is now reduced to the primitive and first simplicity amongst us, and the excrescencies used in the church of Rome are wholly pared away, and by holy prayers and the apostolical ceremony of imposition of the bishop's hands it is worthily and zealously administered. The Latins used to send chrism to the Greeks when they had usurped some jurisdiction over them, and the pope's chaplains went with a quantity of it to C.P. where the Russians usually met them for it; for that was then the ceremony of this ministration: but when the Latins demanded fourscore pounds of gold besides other gifts, they went away, and changed their custom rather than pay an unlawful and ungodly tribute. *Non quærimus vestra, sed vos*; we require nothing but leave to impart God's blessings with pure intentions and a spiritual ministry. And as the bishops of our churches receive nothing from the people for the ministration of this rite, so they desire nothing but love and just obedience in spiritual and ecclesiastical duties; and we offer our flocks spiritual things without mixture of temporal advantages from them; we minister the rituals of the gospel without the inventions of men, religion without superstition, and only desire to be believed in such things which we

---

[7] [Dugdale, Monast. Angl., tom. v. p. 15, from Cotton MSS.]

prove from scripture expounded by the catholic practice of the church of God.

Concerning the subject of this discourse, the Rite of Confirmation, it were easy to recount many great and glorious expressions which we find in the sermons of the holy fathers of the primitive ages: so certain it is that in this thing we ought to be zealous, as being desirous to persuade our people to give us leave to do them great good. But the following pages will do it I hope competently: only we shall remark, that when they had gotten a custom anciently that in cases of necessity they did permit deacons and laymen sometimes to baptize, yet they never did confide in it much, but with much caution and curiosity commanded that such persons should, when that necessity was over, be carried to the bishop to be confirmed, so to supply all precedent defects relating to the past imperfect ministry, and future necessity and danger; as appears in the council of Eliberis.[8] And the ancients had so great estimate and veneration to this holy rite, that as in heraldry they distinguish the same thing by several names when they relate to persons of greater eminency, and they blazon the arms of the gentry by metals, of the nobility by precious stones, but of kings and princes by planets: so when they would signify the unction which was used in confirmation, they gave it a special word, and of more distinction and remark; and therefore the oil used in baptism they called ἔλαιον, but that of confirmation was μυρον καὶ χρίσμα· and they who spake properly kept this difference of words, until by incaution and ignorant carelessness the names fell into confusion, and the thing into disuse and disrespect. But it is no small addition to the honour of this ministration that some wise and good men have piously believed, that when baptized Christians are confirmed and solemnly blessed by the bishop, that then it is that a special angel-guardian is appointed to keep their souls from the assaults of the spirits of darkness. Concerning which though I shall not interpose mine own opinion, yet this I say, that the piety of that supposition is not disagreeable to the intention of this rite: for since by this the Holy Spirit of God (the

---

[8] [Can. 77. tom. i. col. 257.]

Father of spirits) is given, it is not unreasonably thought by them that the other good spirits of God, the angels who are ministering spirits sent forth to minister to the good of them that shall be heirs of salvation, should pay their kind offices in subordination to their prince and fountain; that the first in every kind might be the measure of all the rest. But there are greater and stranger things than this that God does for the souls of His servants, and for the honour of the ministries which Himself hath appointed.

We shall only add that this was ancient, and long before popery entered into the world, and that this rite hath been more abused by popery than by any thing: and to this day the bigots of the Roman church are the greatest enemies to it; and from them the presbyterians. But besides that the church of England and Ireland does religiously retain it, and hath appointed a solemn officer[9] for the ministry; the Lutheran and Bohemian churches do observe it carefully, and it is recommended and established in the Harmony of the Protestant Confessions.

And now may it please your grace to give me leave to implore your aid and countenance for the propagating this so religious and useful a ministry, which, as it is a peculiar of the bishop's office, is also a great enlarger of God's gifts to the people. It is a great instrument of union of hearts, and will prove an effective deletery to schism, and an endearment to the other parts of religion: it is the consummation of baptism, and a preparation to the Lord's supper: it is the virtue from on high, and the solemnity of our spiritual adoption. But there will be no need to use many arguments to enflame your zeal in this affair, when your grace shall find that to promote it will be a great service to God; for this alone will conclude your grace, who are so ready, by laws and executions, by word and by example, to promote the religion of Christ, as it is taught in these churches. I am not confident enough to desire your grace for the reading this discourse to lay aside any one hour of your greater employments, which consume so much of your days and nights: but I say that the subject is greatly worthy of consideration. *Nihil enim inter manus habui,*

---

[9] [sic edd.]

cui majorem sollicitudinem præstare deberem. And for the book itself, I can only say what Secundus[10] did to the wise Lupercus, *Quoties ad fastidium legentium deliciasque respicio, intelligo nobis commendationem ex ipsa mediocritate libri petendam*, 'I can commend it because it is little, and so not very troublesome.' And if it could have been written according to the worthiness of the thing treated in it, it would deserve so great a patronage: but because it is not, it will therefore greatly need it; but it can hope for it on no other account but because it is laid at the feet of a princely person, who is great and good, and one who not only is bound by duty, but by choice hath obliged himself to do advantages to any worthy instrument of religion. But I have detained your grace so long in my address, that your pardon will be all the favour which ought to be hoped for by

your grace's most humble
and obliged servant,
JER. DUNENSIS.

---

[10] [Plin., lib. ii. epist. 5.]

The Introduction

Next to the incarnation of the Son of God and the whole economy of our redemption wrought by Him in an admirable order and conjugation of glorious mercies, the greatest thing that ever God did to the world is the giving to us the Holy Ghost; and possibly this is the consummation and perfection of the other. For in the work of redemption Christ indeed made a new world; we are wholly a new creation, and we must be so: and therefore when S. John began the narrative of the gospel, he began in a manner and style very like to Moses in his history of the first creation; "In the beginning was the Word," &c. "All things were made by Him, and without Him was not any thing made that was made." But as in the creation the matter was first; there were indeed heavens and earth and waters, but all this was rude and "without form," till "the Spirit of God moved upon the face of the waters:" so it is in the new creation. We are a new mass, redeemed with the blood of Christ, rescued from an evil portion and made candidates of heaven and immortality; but we are but an embryo in the regeneration until the Spirit of God enlivens us and moves again upon the waters, and then every subsequent motion and operation is from the Spirit of God. "We cannot say that Jesus is the Lord, but by the Holy Ghost;" by Him we live, in Him we walk, by His aids we pray, by His emotions we desire; we breathe, and sigh, and groan by Him; He 'helps' us in all 'our infirmities,' and He gives us all our strengths; He reveals mysteries to us and teaches us all our duties; He stirs us up to holy desires and He actuates those desires; He "makes us to will and to do of His good pleasure."

For the Spirit of God is that in our spiritual life that a man's soul is in his natural, without it we are but a dead and lifeless trunk. But then as a man's soul in proportion to the several operations of life obtains several appellatives; it is vegetative and nutritive, sensitive and intellective, according as it operates: so is the Spirit of God. He is the spirit of regeneration in baptism, of renovation in repentance; the spirit of love and the spirit of holy fear; the searcher of the hearts and the spirit of discerning; the spirit of wisdom and the spirit of prayer. In one mystery He illuminates and in another He feeds us; He begins in one and finishes and perfects in another. It is the same spirit working divers operations. For He is all this now reckoned and He is everything else that is the principle of good unto us; He is the beginning and the progression, the consummation and perfection of us all; and yet every work of His is perfect in its kind and in order to His own designation, and from the beginning to the end is perfection all the way. Justifying and sanctifying grace is the proper entitative product in all, but it hath divers appellatives and connotations in the several rites; and yet even then also because of the identity of the principle, the similitude and general consonancy in the effect, the same appellative is given, and the same effect imputed to more than one; and yet none of them can be omitted, when the great master of the family hath blessed it and given it institution. Thus S. Dionys[1] calls baptism τὴν ἱερὰν τῆς θεογονίας πλείωσιν, 'the perfection of the divine birth;' and yet the baptized person must receive other mysteries which are more signally perfective: ἡ τοῦ μύρον χρίσις τελειωτική· confirmation is yet more 'perfective,' and is properly the perfection of baptism.

By baptism we are heirs, and are adopted to the inheritance of sons, admitted to the covenant of repentance, and engaged to live a good life; yet this is but the solemnity of the covenant, which must pass into after-acts by other influences of the same divine principle. Until we receive the spirit of obsignation or confirmation, we are but

---

[1] [Eccles. hier., cap. ii. p. 85 C.]

babes in Christ in the meanest sense, infants that can do nothing, that cannot speak, that cannot resist any violence, exposed to every rudeness and perishing by every temptation.

But therefore as God at first appointed us a ministry of a new birth, so also hath He given to His church the consequent ministry of a new strength. The Spirit moved a little upon the waters of baptism, and gave us the principles of life, but in confirmation He makes us able to move ourselves. In the first He is the spirit of life, but in this He is the spirit of strength and motion. *Baptisma est nativitas, unguentum vero est nobis actionis instar et motus*, said Cabasilas.[2] 'In baptism we are intitled to the inheritance; but because we are in our infancy and minority, the father gives unto his sons a tutor, a guardian and a teacher in confirmation,' said Rupertus:[3] that as we are baptized into the death and resurrection of Christ, so in confirmation we may be renewed in the inner man, and strengthened in all our holy vows and purposes by the Holy Ghost ministered according to God's ordinance.

The holy rite of confirmation is a divine ordinance, and it produces divine effects, and is ministered by divine persons, that is, by those whom God hath sanctified and separated to this ministration. At first all that were baptized were also confirmed, and ever since all good people that have understood it have been very zealous for it; and time was in England, even since the first beginnings of the Reformation, when confirmation had been less carefully ministered for about six years, when the people had their first opportunities of it restored, they ran to it in so great numbers that churches and churchyards would not hold them; insomuch that I have read that the bishop of Chester was forced to impose hands on the people in the fields, and was so oppressed with multitudes that he

---

[2] [De vit. in Christo, lib. ii. prop. init.—Magn. biblioth. vet. patr., tom. xiv. p. 106.—'Baptismus enim est generatio sive ortus; ungeuntum sive chrisma actionis et motionis rationem habet.']
[3] De divin. office., 1. v. c. 17. [leg. 16. p. 655.—'Quid prodest si quisquam parentum magnam parvulo conferat hæreditatem, nisi provideat illi tutorem? Paracletus quippe regeneratis in Christo custos et consolator et tutor est,' &c.]

had almost been trod to death by the people, and had died with the throng if he had not been rescued by the civil power.[4]

But men have too much neglected all the ministries of grace, and this most especially, and have not given themselves to a right understanding of it, and so neglected it yet more. But because the prejudice which these parts of the christian church have suffered for want of it is very great (as will appear by enumeration of the many and great blessings consequent to it) I am not without hope that it may be a service acceptable to God, and an useful ministry to the souls of my charges, if by instructing them that know not, and exhorting them that know, I set forward the practice of this holy rite, and give reason why the people ought to love it and to desire it, and how they are to understand and practise it, and consequently with what duteous affections they are to relate to those persons whom God hath in so special and signal manner made to be, for their good and eternal benefit, the ministers of the Spirit and salvation.

S. Bernard,[5] in the life of S. Malachias, my predecessor in the see of Down and Connor, reports that it was the care of that good prelate to renew the rite of confirmation in his diocese, where it had been long neglected and gone into desuetude. It being too much our case in Ireland, I find the same necessity, and am obliged to the same procedure, for the same reason, and in pursuance of so excellent an example. *Hoc est enim evangelizare Christum*, said S. Austin,[6] *non tantum docere quæ sunt dicenda[7] de Christo, sed etiam quæ observanda ei qui accedit ad compagem corporis Christi*, for this is to preach the gospel, not only to teach those things which are to be said of Christ, but those also which are to be observed by every one who desires to be confederated into the society of the body of Christ, which is His church; that is, not only the doctrines of good life, but the mysteries of godliness and the

---

[4] Vindic. ecclesiast. hierarch. per Franc. Hallier. [lib. ii. cap. 5. § 2. p. 125. 4to. Paris. 1632.—è Sandero, schism. Angl., lib. ii.—It may here be mentioned once for all, that Taylor's authorities in this treatise are often taken from Hallier's work; to which therefore reference will sometimes be made in the following notes.]
[5] [col. 1932 K.]
[6] Cap. ix. De fide et operibus. [tom. vi. col. 172.]
[7] [al. 'dicere quæ sunt credenda.']

rituals of religion, which issue from a divine fountain, are to be declared by him who would fully preach the gospel.

In order to which performance I shall declare,

1. The divine original, warranty and institution of the holy rite of confirmation.

2. That this rite was to be a perpetual and never ceasing ministration.

3. That it was actually continued and practised by all the succeeding ages of the purest and primitive churches.

4. That this rite was appropriate to the ministry of bishops.

5. That prayer and imposition of the bishop's hands did make the whole ritual; and though other things were added, yet they were not necessary, or any thing of the institution.

6. That many great graces and blessings were consequent to the worthy reception and due ministration of it.

7. I shall add something of the manner of preparation to it, and reception of it.

Chapter One
Of the divine original, warranty and institution of the holy rite of confirmation.

In the church of Rome they have determined confirmation to be a sacrament *propii nominis*, properly and really; and yet their doctors have, some of them at least, been *paulo iniquiores*, a little unequal and unjust to their proposition, insomuch that from themselves we have had the greatest opposition in this article. Bonacina[1] and Henriquez[2] allow the proposition, but make the sacrament to be so unnecessary that a little excuse may justify the omission and almost neglect of it. And Loëmelius and Daniel à Jesu, and generally the English Jesuits, have, to serve some ends of their own family and order, disputed it almost into contempt, that by representing it as unnecessary, they might do all the ministries ecclesiastical in England without the assistance of bishops their superiors, whom they therefore love not, because they are so. But the theological faculty of Paris have condemned their doctrine as temerarious and savouring of heresy; and in the later schools[3] have approved rather the doctrine of Gamachæus, Estius, Kellison, and Bellarmine, who indeed do follow the doctrine of the most eminent persons in the ancient school, Richard of Armagh, Scotus, Hugo Cavalli, and Gerson the learned chancellor of Paris, who following the old Roman order, Amalarius and Albinus, do all teach confirmation to be of great and pious use,

---

[1] De Sacram., disp. 3. qu. unic. punct. 3. [leg. 2. vid. Hallier, p. 112.]
[2] Lib. 3. De dacram. [i.e. de sacr. confirm., c.i.—Hallier, p. 115.]
[3] [Hallier, p. 116]

of divine original, and to many purposes necessary, according to the doctrine of the scriptures and the primitive church.

Whether confirmation be a sacrament or no, is of no use to dispute; and if it be disputed, it can never be proved to be so as baptism and the Lord's supper, that is, 'as generally necessary to salvation;' but though it be no sacrament, it cannot follow that it is not of very great use and holiness: and as a man is never the less tied to repentance, though it be no sacrament; so neither is he ever the less obliged to receive confirmation, though it be (as it ought) acknowledged to be of an use and nature inferior to the two sacraments of divine, direct and immediate institution. It is certain that the fathers in a large symbolical and general sense call it a sacrament, but mean not the same thing by that word when they apply it to confirmation as they do when they apply it to baptism and the Lord's supper. That it is an excellent and divine ordinance to purposes spiritual, that it comes from God and ministers in our way to God, that is all we are concerned to enquire after: and this I shall endeavour to prove not only against the Jesuits, but against all opponents of what side soever.

1.

My first argument from scripture is what I learn from Optatus and S. Cyril. Optatus[4] writing against the Donatists hath these words, "Christ descended into the water, not that in Him, who is God, was any thing that could be made cleaner, but that the water was to precede the future unction, for the initiating and ordaining and fulfilling the mysteries of baptism. He was washed when He was in the hands of John; then followed the order of the mystery, and the Father finished what the Son did ask, and what the Holy Ghost declared: the heavens were opened, God the Father anointed Him, the spiritual unction presently descended in the likeness of a dove, and sate upon His head, and was spread all over Him, and He was called the Christ when He was the anointed of the Father. To whom also lest imposition of hands should seem to be wanting, the voice of

---

[4] [lib. iv. cap. vii.]

God was heard from the cloud saying, 'This is My Son, in whom I am well pleased; hear ye Him.'" That which Optatus says is this; that upon and in Christ's person, baptism, confirmation and ordination were consecrated and first appointed. He was baptized by S. John; He was confirmed by the Holy Spirit, and anointed with spiritual unction in order to that great work of obedience to His Father's will; and He was consecrated by the voice of God from heaven. In all things Christ is the head and the first-fruits; and in these things was the fountain of the sacraments and spiritual grace, and the great exemplar of the economy of the church. For Christ was *nullius poenitentiæ debitor*;[5] baptism of repentance was not necessary to Him, who never sinned; but so it became Him to fulfil all righteousness, and to be a pattern to us all. But we have need of these things, though He had not; and in the same way in which salvation was wrought by Him for Himself and for us all, in the same way He intended[6] we should walk. He was baptized because His Father appointed it so; we must be baptized because Christ hath appointed it, and we have need of it too. He was consecrated to be the great prophet and the great priest, because "no man takes on him this honour but he that was called of God, as was Aaron:" and all they who are to minister in His prophetical office under Him must be consecrated and solemnly set apart for that ministration, and after His glorious example. He was anointed with a spiritual unction from above after His baptism; for "after Jesus was baptized," He ascended up from the waters, and then the Holy Ghost descended upon Him. It is true He received the fulness of the Spirit; but we receive Him by measure; but "of His fulness we all receive, grace for grace:" that is, all that He received in order to His great work, all that in kind, one for another, grace for grace, we are to receive according to our measures and our necessities. And as all these He received by external ministrations, so must we; God the Father appointed His way, and He by His example first hath appointed the same to us, that we also may 'follow Him in the regeneration,' and 'work out our salvation' by the same graces in the

---

[5] [Tertull. De bapt., cap. xii. p. 299 A.]
[6] 1 John ii. 8 [? 6.]

like solemnities. For if He needed them for Himself, then we need them much more. If He did not need them for Himself, He needed them for us, and for our example, that we might follow His steps, who by receiving these exterior solemnities and inward graces became 'the author and finisher' of our salvation, and the great example of His church. I shall not need to make use of the fancy of the Murcosians and Colabarsians,[7] who turning all mysteries into numbers, reckoned the numeral letters of περιστερὰ, and made them coincident to the α and ω but they intended to say that Christ receiving the holy Dove after His baptism became all in all to us, the beginning and the perfection of our salvation; here He was confirmed, and received the ω to His α, the consummation to His initiation, the completion of His baptism and of His headship in the gospel.—But that which I shall rather add is what S. Cyril[8] from hence argues, "When He truly was baptized in the river of Jordan, He ascended out of the waters, and the Holy Ghost substantially descended upon Him, like resting upon like. And to you also in like manner, after ye have ascended from the waters of baptism, the unction is given, which bears the image or similitude of Him by whom Christ was anointed; that as Christ after baptism and the coming of the Holy Spirit upon Him went forth to battle (in the wilderness) and overcame the adversary; so ye also, after holy baptism and the mystical unction (or confirmation) being vested with the armour of the Holy Spirit, are enabled to stand against the opposite powers." Here then is the first great ground of our solemn receiving the Holy Spirit, or the unction from above after baptism, which we understand and represent by the word confirmation, denoting the principal effect of this unction, spiritual strength. Christ, who is the head of the church, entered this way upon His duty and work, and He who was the first of all the church, the head and great example, is the measure of all the rest, for we can go to heaven no way but in that way in which He went before us.

---

[7] [See Irenaeus, haer., lib. i. cap 13 sq., of the doctrines of Marcus and Colorbasus.]
[8] Cateches. iii. [sc. xxi. seu Mystag. iii. p. 316.] Πνεύματος ἁγίου οὐσιώδης ἐπιφοίτησις αυτώ εγίνετο.

There are some who from this story would infer the descent of the Holy Ghost after Christ's baptism not to signify that confirmation was to be a distinct rite from baptism, but a part of it, yet such a part as gives fulness and consummation to it. S. Hierome, Chrysostom, Euthymius and Theophylact go not so far, but would have us by this to understand that the Holy Ghost is given to them that are baptized. But reason and the context are both against it. 1) Because the Holy Ghost was not given by John's baptism; that was reserved to be one of Christ's glories; who also, when by His disciples He baptized many, did not give them the Holy Ghost; and when He commanded His apostles to baptize all nations, did not at that time so much as promise the Holy Ghost: He was promised distinctly, and given, by another ministration. 2) The descent of the Holy Spirit was a distinct ministry from the baptism; it was not only after Jesus ascended from the waters of baptism, but there was something intervening, and by a new office or ministration, for there was prayer joined in the ministry. So S. Luke observes. "While Jesus was praying, the heavens were opened, and the Holy Spirit descended;" for so Jesus was pleased to consign the whole office and ritual of confirmation: prayer for invocating the Holy Spirit, and giving Him by personal application; which as the Father did immediately, so the bishops do by imposition of hands. 3) S. Austin[9] observes that the apparition of the Holy Spirit like a dove was the visible or ritual part, and the voice of God was the word to make it to be sacramental; *accedit verbum ad elementum, et fit sacramentum*; for so the ministration was not only performed on Christ, but consigned to the church by similitude and exemplar institution.— I shall only add that the force of this argument is established to us by more of the fathers. S. Hilary[10] upon this place hath these words, "The Father's voice was heard, that from those things which were consummated in Christ we might know that after the baptism of water the Holy Spirit from the gates of heaven flies unto us; and that

---

[9] In Joan. tract. lxxx. [tom. iii. part. 2. col. 703 C.]
[10] S. Hilar. can. iv. [leg. ii.] in fine. [col. 617.]

we are to be anointed[11] with the unction of a celestial glory, and be made the sons of God by the adoption of the voice of God, the truth by the very effects of things prefigured unto us the similitude of a sacrament." So S. Chrysostom;[12] "In the beginnings always appears the sensible visions of spiritual things, for their sakes who cannot receive the understanding of an incorporeal nature; that if afterwards they be not so done (that is, after the same visible manner) they may be believed by those things which were already done." But more plain is that of Theophylact,[13] "The Lord had not need of the descent of the Holy Spirit, but He did all things for our sakes; and Himself is become the first fruits of all things which we afterwards were to receive, that He might become the first fruits among many brethren." The consequent is this, which I express in the words of S. Austin,[14] affirming, *Christi in baptismo columbam unctionem nostram præfigurasse*, 'the dove in Christ's baptism did represent and prefigure our unction' from above, that is, the descent of the Holy Ghost upon us in the rite of confirmation. Christ was baptized and so must we: but after baptism He had a new ministration for the reception of the Holy Ghost; and because this was done for our sakes, we also must follow that example. And this being done immediately before His entrance into the wilderness to be tempted of the devil, it plainly describes to us the order of this ministry, and the blessing designed to us: after we are baptized, we need to be strengthened and confirmed *propter pugnam spiritualem*; we are to fight against the flesh, the world and the devil, and therefore must receive the ministration of the Holy Spirit of God: which is the design and proper work of confirmation. "For" (they are the words of the excellent author of the imperfect work upon S. Matthew, imputed to S. Chrysostom[15]) "the baptism of water profits us, because it washes away the sins we have formerly

---

[11] [lat. sic;…'et cœlestis nos gloriæ unctione perfundi, et paternæ vocis adoptione Dei filios fieri; cum ita dispositi in nos sacramenti imaginem ipsis rereum effectibus veritas præfiguraverit.']
[12] In Matthæum. [hom. xii. tom. vii. p. 163 C.]
[13] Ibid. [leg. In Marc. i. 10.]
[14] [vid. in Joan. tract. vi. per tot.—tom. iii. part. 2. col. 330 sqq.]
[15] Homil. iv. [tom. vi. append. p. 38.]

committed, if we repent of them; but it does not sanctify the soul, nor precedes the concupiscences of the heart and our evil thoughts, nor drives them back, nor represses our carnal desires. But he therefore who is (only) so baptized that he does not also receive the Holy Spirit, is baptized in his body, and his sins are pardoned, but in his mind he is yet but a catechumen; for so it is written, 'He that hath not the Spirit of Christ is none of His;' and therefore afterwards out of his flesh will germinate worse sins, because he hath not received the Holy Spirit conserving him (in his baptismal grace) but the house of his body is empty; wherefore that wicked spirit finding it swept with the doctrines of faith as with besoms, enters in, and in a sevenfold manner dwells there." Which words, besides that they well explicate this mystery, do also declare the necessity of confirmation, or receiving the Holy Ghost after baptism, in imitation of the divine precedent of our blessed Saviour.

2.

After the example of Christ, my next argument is from His words spoken to Nicodemus in explication of the prime mysteries evangelical, "Unless a man be born of water and of the Holy Spirit, he shall not enter into the kingdom of God." These words are the great argument which the church uses for the indispensable necessity of baptism; and having in them so great effort, and not being rightly understood, they have suffered many—convulsions shall I call them, or interpretations? Some serve their own hypothesis by saying that water is the symbol, and the spirit is the baptismal grace; others that it is a ἓν διὰ δυοῖν, one is only meant, though here be two signatures: but others conclude that water is only necessary, but the Spirit is super-added as being afterwards to supervene and move upon these waters; and others yet affirm that by water is only meant a spiritual ablution, or the effect produced by the Spirit; and still they have intangled the words so that they have been made useless to the christian church, and the meaning too many things makes nothing to be understood. But truth is easy, intelligible and clear, and without objection, and is plainly this:—

Unless a man be baptized into Christ and confirmed by the Spirit of Christ, he cannot enter into the kingdom of Christ; that is, he is not perfectly adopted into the christian religion, or fitted for the christian warfare. And if this plain and natural sense be admitted, the place is not only easy and intelligible, but consonant to the whole design of Christ and analogy of the New testament; for,

First, our blessed Saviour was catechizing of Nicodemus and teaching him the first rudiments of the gospel, and like a wise master builder first lays the foundation, the doctrines of baptism and laying on of hands; which afterwards S. Paul put into the christian catechism, as I shall shew in the sequel. Now these also are the first principles of the christian religion taught by Christ himself, and things which at least to the doctors might have been so well known, that our blessed Saviour upbraids the not knowing them as a shame to Nicodemus. S. Chrysostom[16] and Theophylact,[17] Euthymius[18] and Rupertus[19] affirm that this generation by water and the Holy Spirit might have been understood by the Old testament in which Nicodemus was so well skilled. Certain it is the doctrine of baptisms was well enough known to the Jews; and the ἐπιφοίτησις τοῦ πνεύματος τοῦ Θεοῦ, the illumination and irradiation's of the Spirit of God was not new to them, who believed the visions and dreams, the 'daughter of a voice,'[20] and the influences from heaven upon the sons of the prophets: and therefore although Christ intended to teach him more than what he had distinct notice of, yet the things themselves had foundation in the law and the prophets: but although they were high mysteries and scarce discerned by them who either were ignorant or incurious of such things; yet to the christians they were the very rudiments of their religion, and are best expounded by observation of what S. Paul placed in the very foundation. But,

Secondly, baptism is the first mystery, that is certain; but that this of being born of the Spirit is also the next, is plain in the very

---

[16] [In Joan. hom. xxvi. tom. viii. p. 151.]
[17] [In loc. p. 594.]
[18] [In loc. tom. iii. p. 101.]
[19] [In loc. tom. ii. p. 247.]
[20] [בַּת קוֹל —See Buxtorf in בָּנָה]

order of the words: and that it does mean a mystery distinct from baptism, will be easily assented to by them who consider, that although Christ baptized and made many disciples by the ministry of His apostles, yet they who were so baptized into Christ's religion did not receive this baptism of the Spirit till after Christ's ascension.

Thirdly, the baptism of water was not peculiar to John the baptist, for it was also of Christ and ministered by His command; it was common to both, and therefore the baptism of water is the less principal here: something distinct from it is here intended. Now if we add to these words, that S. John tells of another baptism which was Christ's peculiar, "He shall baptize you with the Holy Ghost and with fire;" that these words were literally verified upon the apostles in Pentecost, and afterwards upon all the baptized in spiritual effect, who besides the baptism of water distinctly had the baptism of the spirit in confirmation; it will follow that of necessity this must be the meaning and the verification of these words of our blessed Saviour to Nicodemus, which must mean a double baptism: *transibimus per aquam et ignem antequam veniemus in refrigerium*, 'we must pass through water and fire before we enter into rest;' that is, we must first be baptized with water and then with the Holy Ghost, who first descended in fire; that is, the only way to enter into Christ's kingdom is by these two doors of the 'tabernacle which God hath pitched and not man,' first by baptism, and then by confirmation; first by water, and then by the Spirit.

The primitive church had this notion so fully amongst them, that the author of the apostolical constitutions attributed to S. Clement,[21] who was S. Paul's scholar, affirms that a man is made a perfect christian (meaning ritually and sacramentally, and by all exterior solemnity) by the water of baptism and confirmation of the bishop, and from these words of Christ now alleged derives the use and institution of the rite of confirmation. The same sense of these words is given to us by S. Cyprian,[22] who intending to prove the

---

[21] S. Clem. ep. iv. [ad Julium et Julianum. fol. 76. ed. fol. Par. 1544.]—Constit. apost. [lib. iii. cap. 17.]

[22] Ad Stephanum. [ep. lxxxii. p. 196.]

insufficiency of one without the other, says, *Tunc enim plene sanctificari et esse Dei filii possunt si sacramento utroque nascantur, cum scriptum sit, Nisi quis natus fuerit ex aqua et Spiritui non potest intrare in regnum Dei*, 'then they may be fully sanctified and become the sons of God, if they be born with both the sacraments or rites; for it is written, 'Unless a man be born of water and the Spirit, he cannot enter into the kingdom of God.'" The same also is the commentary of Eusebius Emissenus;[23] and S. Austin[24] tells that although some understand these words only of baptism, and others of the Spirit only, viz. in confirmation; yet others (and certainly much better) understand *utrumque sacramentum*, 'both the mysteries,' of confirmation as well as baptism. Amalarius Fortunatus[25] brings this very text to reprove them that neglect the episcopal imposition of hands; "Concerning them who by negligence lose the bishop's presence, and receive not the imposition of his hands, it is to be considered, lest in justice they be condemned, in which they exercise justice negligently, because they ought to make haste to the imposition of hands; because Christ said, 'Unless a man be born again of water and the Spirit, he cannot enter into the kingdom of God:' and as He said this, so also He said, 'Unless your righteousness exceed the righteousness of the scribes and pharisees, ye shall not enter into the kingdom of heaven.'"

To this I foresee two objections may be made.

First, that Christ did not institute confirmation in this place, because confirmation being for the gift of the Holy Ghost, who was to come upon none of the apostles till Jesus was glorified, these words seem too early for the consigning an effect that was to be so long after, and a rite that could not be practised till many intermedial events should happen. So said the evangelist,[26] "The Holy Ghost was come upon none of them, because Jesus was not yet glorified;" intimating that this great effect was to be in after-time: and it is not likely that the ceremony should be ordained before the effect itself was ordered and provided for; that the solemnity should be appointed

---

[23] Homil. in dominic. prim. post Ascens. [p. 687 sqq.]
[24] Epist. cviii. [al. cclxv.] ad Seleucianum. [tom. ii. col. 896.]
[25] Lib. i. c. 27. [p. 322.]
[26] [John vii. 39.]

before provisions were made for the mystery; and that the outward, which was wholly for the inward, should be instituted before the inward and principal had its abode amongst us.

To this I answer, first, that it is no unusual thing; for Christ gave the sacrament of His body before His body was given; the memorial of His death was instituted before His death.—Secondly, confirmation might here as well be instituted as baptism, and by the same reason that the church from these words concludes the necessity of one, she may also infer the designation of the other; for the effect of baptism was at that time no more produced than that of confirmation. Christ had not yet purchased to Himself a church, He had not wrought remission of sins to all that believe on Him; the death of Christ was not yet passed, into which death the christian church was to be baptized.—Thirdly, these words are so an institution of confirmation, as the sixth chap. of S. John is of the blessed eucharist: it was *designativa*, not *ordinativa*, it was in design, not in present command; here it was preached, but not reducible to practice till its proper season.—Fourthly, it was like the words of Christ to S. Peter, "When thou art converted, confirm thy brethren:" here the command was given, but that confirmation of his brethren was to be performed in a time relative to a succeeding accident. Fifthly, it is certain that long before the event and grace was given, Christ did speak of the spirit of confirmation, that spirit which was to descend in Pentecost, which all they were to receive who should believe on Him, which whosoever did receive, out of his belly should flow rivers of living waters, as is to be read in that place of S. John[27] now quoted.—Sixthly, this predesignation of the holy spirit of confirmation was presently followed by some little antepast and *donariola*, or little givings of the Spirit; for our blessed Saviour gave the Holy Ghost three several times. First ἀμυδρῶς,[28] 'obscurely' and by intimation and secret virtue, then when He sent them to heal the sick and anoint them with oil in the name of the Lord. Secondly, ἐκτυποτέρως, 'more expressly' and signally after the resurrection,

---

[27] [Chap. vii. 38.]
[28] [Greg. Naz. ut in not. 31, infra.]

when He took His leave of them, and said, "Receive ye the Holy Ghost;" and this was to give them a power of ministering remission of sins, and therefore related to baptism and the ministries of repentance. But thirdly, He gave it τελειοτέρως, 'more perfectly,' and this was the spirit of confirmation; for He 'was not at all until now,' οὔπω γὰρ ἦν πνεῦμα ἅγιον, says the text, 'the Holy Ghost was not yet:' so almost all the Greek copies printed and manuscript; and so S. Chrysostom, Athanasius, Cyril, Ammonius in the Catena of the Greeks, Leontius, Theophylact, Euthymius, and all the Greek fathers read it; so S. Hierome[29] and S. Austin[30] among the Latins, and some Latin translations read it. Our translations read it, 'the Holy Ghost was not yet given,' was not ἐν αὐτοῖς, 'in them,' as some few Greek copies read it: but the meaning is alike, confirmation was not yet actual, the Holy Spirit, viz. of confirmation, was not yet come upon the church: but it follows not but He was long before promised, designed and appointed, spoken of and declared. The first of these collations had the ceremony of chrism or anointing joined with it, which the church in process of time transferred into her use and ministry: yet it is the last only that Christ passed into an ordinance for ever; it is this only which is the sacramental consummation of our regeneration in Christ; for in this the Holy Spirit is not only ἐνεργείᾳ παρὸν, 'present by His power,' but present οὐσιωδῶς, ὡς ἄν εἴποι τις συγγινόμενόν τε καὶ πολιτευόμενον, as S. Gregory Nazianzen[31] expresses it, to dwell with us, to converse with us, and to abide for ever; οὗ ἐξέχεε ἐφ' ἡμᾶς πλουσίως· so S. Paul describes this spirit of confirmation, the spirit which He hath poured forth upon us richly or plentifully, that is, in great measures, and to the full consummation of the first mysteries of our regeneration. Now because Christ is the great fountain of this blessing to us, and He it was who sent His Father's spirit upon the church, Himself best knew His own intentions, and the great blessings He intended to communicate to His church, and therefore it was most agreeable that from His

---

[29] Qu. ix. ad Hedibiam. [tom. iv. part. I. col. 179.]
[30] In Joan., tract. xxij. [leg. xxxii. tom. iii. part. 2. col. 526.—But both authors have 'Nondum erat Spiritus datus.']
[31] [Orat. xli. cap. 11. tom. i. p. 740 A.]

sermons we should learn His purposes and His blessing, and our duty. Here Christ declared *rem sacramenti*, the spiritual grace which He would afterwards impart to His church by exterior ministry, in this as in all other graces, mysteries and rituals evangelical: *Nisi quis*, 'unless a man be born both of water and the Spirit, he cannot enter into the kingdom of God.'

But the next objection is yet more material; for,

Secondly, if this be the meaning of our blessed Saviour, then confirmation is as necessary as baptism, and without it ordinarily no man can be saved. The solution of this will answer a case of conscience, concerning the necessity of confirmation; and in what degree of duty and diligence we are bound to take care that we receive this holy rite. I answer therefore, that entering into the kingdom of God is being admitted into the christian church and warfare, to become sons of God, and soldiers of Jesus Christ. And though this be the outward door and the first entrance into life, and consequently the king's high-way and the ordinary means of salvation; yet we are to distinguish the external ceremony from the internal mystery: the *Nisi quis* is for this, not for that; and yet that also is the ordinary way. Unless a man be baptized, that is, unless he be indeed regenerate, he cannot be saved: and yet baptism, or the outward washing, is the solemnity and ceremony of its ordinary ministration, and he that neglects this when it may be had is not indeed regenerate; he is not renewed in the spirit of his mind, because he neglects God's way, and therefore can as little be saved as he who, having received the external sacrament, puts a bar to the intromission of the inward grace. Both cannot always be had; but when they can, although they are not equally valuable in the nature of the thing, yet they are made equally necessary by the divine commandment. And in this there is a great but general mistake in the doctrine of the schools, disputing concerning what sacraments are necessary *necessitate medii*, that is, as necessary means, and what are necessary by the necessity of precept or divine commandment. For although a less reason will excuse from the actual susception of some than of others, and a less diligence for the obtaining of one will serve than in obtaining of another, and a supply in one is easier obtained than in another; yet no sacrament hath in it any other necessity than what is made merely by the divine commandment: but the grace of every sacrament or rite of mystery which is of divine ordinance is necessary indispensably, so as without it no man can be saved. And this difference is highly remarkable in the words of Christ recorded by S. Mark,[32] "He that believeth and is baptized shall be saved, but he that believeth not shall be damned." Baptism itself, as to the external part, is not necessary *necessitate medii*, or indispensably; but baptismal faith for the remission of sins in persons capable, that indeed is necessary: for Christ does not say that the want of baptism damns as the want of faith does; and yet both baptism and faith are the ordinary way of salvation, and both necessary; baptism because it is so by the divine commandment, and faith as a necessary means of salvation, in the very economy and dispensation of the gospel. Thus it is also in the other sacrament, "Unless we eat the flesh of the Son of man and drink His blood we have no life in us,"[33] and yet God forbid that every man that is not communicated should die eternally. But it means plainly that without receiving Christ, as He is by God's intention intended we should receive Him in the communion, we have no life in us; plainly thus,— Without the internal grace we cannot live, and the external ministry is the usual and appointed means of conveying to us the internal; and therefore although without the external it is possible to be saved when it is impossible to be had, yet with the wilful neglect of it we cannot. Thus therefore we are to understand the words of Christ declaring the necessity of both these ceremonies; they are both necessary, because they are the means of spiritual advantages and graces, and both minister to the proper ends of their appointment, and both derive from a divine original; but the ritual or ceremonial part in rare emergencies is dispensable, but the grace is indispensable. Without the grace of baptism we shall die in our sins; and without the grace or internal part of confirmation we shall never be able to resist the devil, but shall be taken captive by him at his will. Now the external or ritual part is the means, the season and opportunity of this grace; and

---

[32] [Mark xvi. 16.]
[33] John vi. [53.]

therefore is at no hand to be neglected, lest we be accounted despisers of the grace, and tempters of God to ways and provisions extraordinary. For although when without our fault we receive not the sacramental part, God can and will supply it to us out of His own stores, because no man can perish without his own fault, and God can permit to Himself what He pleases, as being Lord of the grace and of the sacrament; yet to us He hath given a law and a rule, and that is the way of His church in which all christians ought to walk. In short, the use of it is greatly profitable, the neglect is inexcusable, but the contempt is damnable. *Tenentur non negligere si pateat opportunitas*, said the bishops in a synod at Paris,[34] 'If there be an opportunity it must not be neglected.' *Obligantur suscipere, aut saltem non contemnere*, said the synod at Sens,[35] 'They are bound to receive it, or at least not to despise it.' Now he despises it that refuses it when he is invited to it or when it is offered, or that neglects it without cause; for causelessly and contemptuously are all one. But these answers were made by gentle casuists; he only values the grace that desires it, that longs for it, that makes use of all the means of grace, that seeks out for the means, that refuses no labour, that goes after them as the merchant goes after gain: and therefore the old *Ordo Romanus*[36] admonishes more strictly, *Omnino præcavendum esse ut hoc sacramentum confirmationis non negligatur, quia tunc omne baptisma legitimum christianitatis nomine confirmatur,* 'we must by all means take heed that the rite of confirmation be not neglected, because in that every true baptism is ratified and confirmed.' Which words are also to the same purpose made use of by Albinus Flaccus.[37] No man can tell to what degrees of diligence and labour, to what sufferings or journeyings he is obliged for the procuring of this ministry: there must be *debita sollicitudo*; a real providential zealous care to be where it is to be had, is the duty of every christian according to his own circumstances; but they who will not receive it unless it be brought to their doors, may

---

[34] [Bochell. decret. Eccles. Gall.—vid. Hallier, p. 116.]
[35] [Ibid.]
[36] In office. sab. Pasch. post orat. quæ dicitur 'Data confirm.' [In biblioth. vett. patr., tom. viii. p. 434.]
[37] [al. Alcuinus.] De offic. divin. in sabb. S. Pasch. [col. 1064 A.]

live in such places and in such times where they shall be sure to miss it and pay the price of their neglect of so great a ministry of salvation. *Turpissima est jactura quæ per negligentiam fit,*[38] 'he is a fool that loses his good by carelessness:' but no man is zealous for his soul, but he who not only omits no opportunity of doing it advantage when it is ready for him, but makes and seeks and contrives opportunities. *Si non necessitate, sed incuria et voluntate remanserit,* as S. Clement's expression is; if a man wants it by necessity, it may by the overflowings of the divine grace be supplied, but not so if negligence or choice causes the omission.

3.

Our way being made plain, we may proceed to other places of scripture to prove the divine original of confirmation. It was a plant of our heavenly Father's planting, it was a branch of the vine, and how it springs from the root Christ Jesus we have seen; it is yet more visible as it was dressed and cultivated by the apostles. Now as soon as the apostles had received the Holy Spirit, they preached and baptized, and the inferior ministers did the same, and S. Philip particularly did so at Samaria, the converts of which place received all the fruits of baptism; but christians though they were, they wanted a τελείωσις, something to make them perfect. The other part of the narrative I shall set down in the words of S. Luke:[39] "Now when the apostles which were at Jerusalem heard that Samaria had received the word of God, they sent unto them Peter and John; who, when they were come down, prayed for them that they might receive the Holy Ghost: for as yet He was fallen upon none of them, only they were baptized in the name of the Lord Jesus. Then laid they their hands on them, and they received the Holy Ghost." If it had not been necessary to have added a new solemnity and ministration, it is not to be supposed the apostles Peter and John would have gone from Jerusalem to impose hands on the baptized at Samaria. *Id quod deerat a Petro et Joanne factum est, ut oratione pro eis habita et manu imposita,*

---

[38] Seneca [so Hallier, p. 177.]
[39] [Acts viii. 14-17.]

invocaretur et infunderetur super eos Spiritus Sanctus, said S. Cyprian;[40] it was not necessary that they should be baptized again, only 'that which was wanting was performed by Peter and John, that by prayer and imposition of hands the Holy Ghost should be invocated and poured upon them.' The same also is from this place affirmed by P. Innocentius the first,[41] S. Hierome, and many others: and in the Acts of the apostles we find another instance of the celebration of this ritual and mystery, for it is signally expressed of the baptized Christians at Ephesus, that S. Paul first baptized them, and then laid his hands on them, and they received the Holy Ghost. And these testimonies are the great warranty for this holy rite. *Quod nunc in confirmandis neophytis manus impositio tribuit singulis, hoc tunc Spiritus Sancti descensio in credentium populo donavit universis*, said Eucherius[42] Lugdunensis, in his homily of Pentecost: the same thing that is done now in imposition of hands on single persons, is no other than that which was done upon all believers in the descent of the Holy Ghost; it is the same ministry, and all deriving from the same authority.

Confirmation or imposition of hands for the collation of the Holy Spirit we see was actually practised by the apostles, and that even before and after they preached the gospel to the gentiles; and therefore Amalarius,[43] who entered not much into the secret of it, reckons this ritual as derived from the apostles *per consuetudinem*, 'by catholic custom;' which although it is not perfectly spoken as to the whole αὐθεντία or authority of it, yet he places it in the apostles, and is a witness of the catholic succeeding custom and practice of the church of God. Which thing also Zanchius observing, though he followed the sentiment of Amalarius, and seemed to understand no more of it, yet says well, *Interim* (says he) *exempla apostolorum et veteris ecclesiæ vellem pluris æstimari*, 'I wish that the example of the apostles and the primitive church were of more value amongst Christians.' It were very well indeed they were so, but there is more in it than mere example. These examples of such solemnities productive of such

---

[40] Ad Jubaian. [ep. lxxiii. p. 202.]
[41] Epist. i. c. 3. adv. Luciferian. [tom. iv. part. 2. col. 294.]
[42] [Sive Eusebius Lugd.—Magn. bibl. vett. patr., tom. v. part. 1. p. 572 A.]
[43] [lib. i. c. 27. p. 324 B.]

spiritual effects are, as S. Cyprian calls them, *apostolica magisteria*, the apostles are our masters in them, and have given rules and precedents for the church to follow. This is a christian law, and written as all scriptures are, for our instruction. But this I shall expressly prove in the next paragraph.

4.

We have seen the original from Christ, the practice and exercise of it in the apostles and the first converts in christianity; that which I shall now remark is, that this is established and passed into a christian doctrine. The warranty for what I say is the words of S. Paul,[44] where the holy rite of confirmation, so called from the effect of this ministration, and expressed by the ritual part of it, imposition of hands, is reckoned a fundamental point, θεμέλιος ἐπιθέσεως χειρῶν· "Not laying again the foundation of repentance from dead works and of faith towards God, of the doctrine of baptisms, and of laying on of hands, of resurrection from the dead, and eternal judgment." Here are six fundamental points of S. Paul's catechism, which he laid as the foundation or the beginning of the institution of the christian church; and among these imposition of hands is reckoned as a part of the foundation, and therefore they who deny it dig up foundations. Now that this imposition of hands is that which the apostles used in confirming the baptized, and invocating the Holy Ghost upon them, remains to be proved.

For it is true that imposition of hands signifies all christian rites except baptism and the Lord's supper; not the sacraments, but all the sacramentals of the church: it signifies confirmation, ordination, absolution, visitation of the sick, blessing single persons (as Christ did the children brought to Him) and blessing marriages; all these were usually ministered by imposition of hands. Now the three last are not pretended to be any part of this foundation; neither reason, authority, nor the nature of the thing suffer any such pretension: the question then is between the first three.

---

[44] [Heb. vi. 1, 2.]

First, absolution of penitents cannot be meant here, not only because we never read that the apostles did use that ceremony in their absolutions; but because the apostle speaking of the foundation in which baptism is, and is reckoned one of the principal parts in the foundation, there needed no absolution but baptismal, for they and we believing 'one baptism for the remission of sins,'[45] this is all the absolution that can be at first and in the foundation. The other was *secunda post naufragium tabula*, it came in after, when men had made a shipwreck of their good conscience, and were, as S. Peter[46] says, λήθην λαβόντες τοῦ καθαρισμοῦ τῶν πάλαι αὐτῶν ἁμαρτιῶν, 'forgetful of the former cleansing and purification and washing of their old sins.'

Secondly, it cannot be meant of ordination; and this is also evident, 1) Because the apostle says he would thenceforth leave to speak of the foundation, and go on to perfection, that is, to higher mysteries; now in rituals, of which he speaks, there is none higher than ordination. 2) The apostle, saying he would speak no more of imposition of hands, goes presently to discourse of the mysteriousness of the evangelical priesthood, and the honour of that vocation; by which it is evident he spake nothing of ordination in the catechism or narrative of fundamentals. 3) This also appears from the context, not only because laying on of hands is immediately set after baptism, but also because in the very next words of his discourse he does enumerate and apportion to baptism and confirmation their proper and proportioned effects: to baptism, 'illumination,' according to the perpetual style of the church of God, calling baptism φωτισμὸν, 'an enlightening;' and to confirmation he reckons 'tasting the heavenly gift,' and being made partakers of the Holy Ghost; by the thing signified declaring the sign, and by the mystery the rite. Upon these words S. Chrysostom[47] discoursing, says that "all these are fundamental articles; that is, that we ought to repent from dead works, to be baptized into the faith of Christ, and be made worthy of the gift of the Spirit, who is given by imposition of hands, and we are

---

[45] Symbol. Nicæn. et C. P.
[46] [2. Pet. i. 9.]
[47] [In Hebr. vi. hom. ix. tom. xii. p. 93.]

to be taught the mysteries of the resurrection and eternal judgment." This catechism (says he) is perfect: so that if any man have faith in God, and being baptized is also confirmed, and so tastes the heavenly gift and partakes of the Holy Ghost, and by hope of the resurrection tastes of the good things of the world to come, if he falls away from this state, and turns apostate from this whole dispensation, digging down and turning up these foundations, he shall never be built again; he can never be baptized again, and never be confirmed anymore; God will not begin again, and go over with him again, he cannot be made a Christian twice: if he remains upon these foundations, though he sins he may be renewed διὰ μετάνοιαν, 'by repentance,' and by a resuscitation of the Spirit, if he have not wholly quenched Him; but if he renounces the whole covenant, disown and cancel these foundations, he is desperate, he can never be renewed εἰς μετάνοιαν, 'to the title and economy of repentance.' This is the full explication of this excellent place, and any other ways it cannot reasonably be explicated: but therefore into this place any notice of ordination cannot come, no sense, no mystery can be made of it or drawn from it; but by the interposition of confirmation the whole context is clear, rational, and intelligible.

This then is that imposition of hands of which the apostle speaks. *Unus hic locus abunde testatur, &c.*, saith Calvin,[48] 'this one place doth abundantly witness' that the original of this rite or ceremony was from the apostles; οὕτω γὰρ τὸ πνεῦμα ἐλάμβανον, saith S. Chrysostom,[49] for by this rite of imposition of hands they received the Holy Ghost. For though the Spirit of God was given extra-regularly, and at all times, as God was pleased to do great things; yet this imposition of hands was διακονία πνεύματος, this was the ministry of the Spirit. For so we receive Christ when we hear and obey His word, we eat Christ by faith, and we live by His spirit; and yet the blessed eucharist is διακονία σώματος καὶ αἵματος, 'the ministry of the body and blood of Christ.' Now as the Lord's supper is appointed ritually to convey Christ's body and blood to us; so is confirmation

---

[48] [In Heb. vi. 2.]
[49] In hunc locum. [hom. ix. tom. xii. p. 95 C.]

ordained ritually to give unto us the Spirit of God. And though by accident and by the overflowings of the Spirit it may come to pass that a man does receive perfective graces alone, and without ministries external: yet such a man without a miracle is not a perfect Christian *ex statuum vitæ dispositione*; but in the ordinary ways and appointment of God, and until he receive this imposition of hands, and be confirmed, is to be accounted an imperfect Christian. But of this afterwards.

I shall observe one thing more out of this testimony of S. Paul. He calls it the doctrine of baptisms and laying on of hands: by which it does not only appear to be a lasting ministry, because no part of the christian doctrine could change or be abolished; but hence also it appears to be of divine institution. For if it were not, S. Paul had been guilty of that which our blessed Saviour reproves in the scribes and pharisees, and should have taught for doctrines the commandments of men. Which because it cannot be supposed, it must follow that this doctrine of confirmation or imposition of hands is apostolical and divine. The argument is clear and not easy to be reproved.

Chapter Two
The rite of confirmation is a perpetual and never-ceasing ministry.

Yea, but what is this to us? It belonged to the days of wonder and extraordinary; the Holy Ghost breathed upon the apostles and apostolical men, but then He breathed His last; *recedente gratia recessit disciplina*, 'when the grace departed we had no further use of ceremony.'—In answer to this I shall ψιλαῖς ἐπινοίαις, by divers particulars evince plainly, that this ministry of confirmation was not temporary and relative only to the acts of the apostles, but was to descend to the church for ever. This indeed is done already in the preceding section, in which it is clearly manifested that Christ himself[1] made the baptism of the Spirit to be necessary to the church. He declared the fruits of this baptism, and did particularly relate it to the descent of the Holy Spirit upon the church at and after that glorious Pentecost. He sanctified it and commended it by His example; just as in order to baptism He sanctified the flood Jordan, and all other waters, to the mystical washing away of sin, viz., by His great example, and fulfilling this righteousness also. This doctrine the apostles first found in their own persons and experience, and practised to all their converts after baptism by a solemn and external rite; and all this passed into an evangelical doctrine, the whole mystery being signified by the external rite in the words of the apostle, as before it was by Christ expressing only the internal; so that there needs no more strength to this argument.

---

[1] [John iii. 5.]

But that there may be wanting no moments to this truth which the holy scripture affords, I shall add more weight to it: and,

1. The perpetuity of this holy rite appears, because this great gift of the Holy Ghost was promised to abide with the church for ever. And when the Jews heard the apostles speak with tongues at the first and miraculous descent of the Spirit in Pentecost, to take off the strangeness of the wonder and the envy of the power, S. Peter[2] at that very time tells them plainly, "Repent and be baptized every one of you, .. and ye shall receive the gift of the Holy Ghost," ἕκαστος ὑμῶν· not the meanest person amongst you all but shall receive this great thing which ye observe us to have received; and not only you but your children too; not your children of this generation only,

> Sed nati natorum, et qui nascentur ab illis,

but your children for ever: "For the promise is to you and to your children, and to all that are afar off, even to as many as the Lord our God shall call."[3] Now then let it be considered,

1) This gift is by promise; by a promise not made to the apostles alone, but to all; to all for ever.

2) Consider here at the very first, as there is a *verbum*, a word of promise, so there is *sacramentum* too (I use the word, as I have already premonished, in a large sense only, and according to the style of the primitive church:) it is a rite partly moral, partly ceremonial; the first is prayer, and the other is laying on of the hands: and to an effect that is but transient and extraordinary and of a little abode, it is not easy to be supposed that such a solemnity should be appointed. I say such a solemnity; that is, it is not imaginable that a solemn rite annexed to a perpetual promise should be transient and temporary, for by the nature of relatives they must be of equal abode. The promise is of a thing for ever; the ceremony or rite was annexed to the promise, and therefore this also must be for ever.

---

[2] [Acts ii. 38.]
[3] [ver. 39.]

3) This is attested by S. Paul,[4] who reduces this argument to this mystery, saying, "In whom after that ye believed, *signati estis Spiritu sancto promissionis*, ye were sealed by that holy Spirit of promise." He spake it to the Ephesians, who well understood his meaning by remembering what was done to themselves by the apostles[5] but a while before, who after they had baptized them did lay their hands upon them, and so they were sealed, and so they received the holy Spirit of promise; for here the very matter of fact is the clearest commentary on S. Paul's words: the Spirit which was promised to all Christians they then received when they were consigned, or had the ritual seal of confirmation by imposition of hands. One thing I shall remark here, and that is, that this and some other words of scripture relating to the sacraments or other rituals of religion do principally mean the internal grace, and our consignation is by a secret power, and the work is within; but it does not therefore follow that the external rite is not also intended: for the rite is so wholly for the mystery, and the outward for the inward, and yet by the outward God so usually and regularly gives the inward, that as no man is to rely upon the external ministry as if the *opus operatum* would do the whole duty, so no man is to neglect the external because the internal is the more principal. The mistake in this particular hath caused great contempt of the sacraments and rituals of the church, and is the ground of the Socinian errors in these questions. But,

4) What hinders any man from a quick consent at the first representation of these plain reasonings and authorities? Is it because there were extraordinary effects accompanying this ministration, and because now there are not, that we will suppose the whole economy must cease? If this be it, and indeed this is all that can be supposed in opposition to it, it is infinitely vain.

1) Because these extraordinary effects did continue even after the death of all the apostles. S. Irenæus[6] says they did continue even to his time, even the greatest instance of miraculous power; *Et in*

---

[4] [Eph. i. 13.]
[5] [Acts xix. 6.]
[6] Lib. ii. cap. 57. [al. 31. p. 164.]

fraternitate sæpissime propter aliquid necessarium, ea quæ est in quoquo loco universa ecclesia postulante per jejunium et supplicationem multam, reversus est spiritus, &c., 'when God saw it necessary, and the church prayed and fasted much, they did miraculous things, even of reducing the spirit to a dead man.'

2) In the days of the apostles the Holy Spirit did produce miraculous effects, but neither always, nor at all in all men: "are all workers of miracles? do all speak with tongues? do all interpret? can all heal?"[7] No, the Spirit bloweth where He listeth, and as He listeth; He gives gifts to all, but to some after this manner and to some after that.

3) These gifts were not necessary at all times any more than to all persons; but the promise did belong to all, and was made to all, and was performed to all. In the days of the apostles there was an effusion of the Spirit of God, it ran over, it was for themselves and others, it wet the very ground they trod upon, and made it fruitful; but it was not to all in like manner, but there was also then, and since then, a diffusion of the Spirit, *tanquam in pleno.* S. Stephen was full of the Holy Ghost, he was full of faith and power:[8] the Holy Ghost was given to him to fulfil his faith principally, the working miracles was but collateral and incident. But there is also an infusion of the Holy Ghost, and that is to all, and that is for ever: "the manifestation of the Spirit is given to every man to profit withal,"[9] saith the apostle. And therefore if the grace be given to all, there is no reason that the ritual ministration of that grace should cease, upon pretence that the Spirit is not given extraordinarily.

4) These extraordinary gifts were indeed at first necessary. "In the beginnings always appear the sensible visions of spiritual things for their sakes who cannot receive the understanding of an incorporeal nature, that if afterward they be not so done they may be believed by those things which were already done," said S. Chrysostom[10] in the place before quoted; that is, these visible

---

[7] [1 Cor. xii. 29.]
[8] [Acts vi. 8.]
[9] [1 Cor. xii. 7.]
[10] In Matthæum. [Chapter One, note 12., supra.]

appearances were given at first by reason of the imperfection of the state of the church, but the greater gifts were to abide for ever: and therefore it is observable that S. Paul says that the gift of tongues is one of the least and most useless things; a mere sign, and not so much as a sign to believers, but to infidels and unbelievers; and before this he greatly prefers the gift of prophesying or preaching, which yet all Christians know does abide with the church for ever.

5) To every ordinary and perpetual ministry at first there were extraordinary effects and miraculous consignations. We find great parts of nations converted at one sermon. Three thousand converts came in at once preaching of S. Peter, and five thousand at another sermon: and persons were miraculously cured by the prayer of the bishop in his visitation of a sick Christian; and devils cast out in the conversion of a sinner; and blindness cured at the baptism of S. Paul; and Æneas was healed of a palsy at the same time he was cured of his infidelity; and Eutychus was restored to life at the preaching of S. Paul. And yet that now we see no such extraordinaries, it follows not that the visitation of the sick, and preaching sermons, and absolving penitents are not ordinary and perpetual ministrations: and therefore to fancy that invocation of the Holy Spirit and imposition of hands is to cease when the extraordinary and temporary contingencies of it are gone, is too trifling a fancy to be put in balance against so sacred an institution relying upon so many scriptures.

6) With this objection some vain persons would have troubled the church in S. Austin's time; but he considered it with much indignation, writing against the Donatists. His words are these,[11] "At the first times the Holy Spirit fell upon the believers, and they spake with tongues which they had not learned, according as the Spirit gave them utterance. They were signs fitted for the season; for so the Holy Ghost ought to have signified in all tongues, because the gospel of God was to run through all the nations and languages of the world: so it was signified, and so it passed through. But is it therefore expected that they upon whom there is imposition of hands that they

---

[11] Tract. vi. in [epist.] canonicam Joan. circa med. [§10 . tom . iii. part. 2. col. 868.] et lib. iii. [de Bapt.] contr. Donat. c. 6. [leg. 16. tom. ix. col. 116 F.]

might receive the Holy Ghost, that they should speak with tongues? or when we lay hands on infants, does every one of you attend to hear them speak with tongues, and when he sees that they do not speak with tongues is any of you of so perverse a heart as to say they have not received the Holy Ghost, for if they had received Him they would speak with tongues as it was done at first? But if by these miracles there is not now given any testimony of the presence of the Holy Spirit, how doth any one know that he hath received the Holy Ghost?" *Interroget cor suum si diligit fratrem, manet Spiritus Dei in illo.* It is true the gift of tongues doth not remain, but all the greater gifts of the Holy Spirit remain with the church for ever; sanctification and power, fortitude and hope, faith and love. Let every man search his heart, and see if he belongs to God; whether the love of God be not spread in his heart by the Spirit of God: let him see if he be not patient in troubles, comforted in his afflictions, bold to confess the faith of Christ crucified, zealous of good works. These are the miracles of grace, and the mighty powers of the Spirit, according to that saying of Christ,[12] "These signs shall follow them that believe; in My name shall they cast out devils, they shall speak with new tongues, they shall tread on serpents, they shall drink poison and it shall not hurt them, and they shall lay their hands on the sick and they shall recover." That which we call the miraculous part is the less power; but to cast out the devil of lust, to throw down the pride of Lucifer, to tread on the great dragon, and to triumph over our spiritual enemies, to cure a diseased soul, to be unharmed by the poison of temptation, of evil examples and evil company: these are the true signs that shall follow them that truly and rightly believe on the name of the Lord Jesus; this is to live in the Spirit, and to walk in the Spirit; this is more than to receive the Spirit to a power of miracles and supernatural products in a natural matter: for this is from a supernatural principle to receive supernatural aids to a supernatural end in the diviner spirit of a man; and this being more miraculous than the other, it ought not to be pretended that the discontinuance of extraordinary miracles should

---

[12] [Mark xvi. 17.]

cause the discontinuance of an ordinary ministration; and this is that which I was to prove.

7) To which it is not amiss to add this observation, that Simon Magus offered to buy this power of the apostles, that he also by laying on of hands might thus minister the Spirit. Now he began this sin in the christian church, and it is too frequent at this day: but if all this power be gone, then nothing of that sin can remain; if the subject matter be removed, then the appendent crime cannot abide, and there can be no simony, so much as by participation; and whatever is or can be done in this kind, is no more of this crime than drunkenness is of adultery; it relates to it, or may be introductive of it, or be something like it. But certainly since the church is not so happy as to be entirely free from the crime of simony, it will be hard to say that the power the buying of which was the principle of this sin, and therefore the rule of all the rest, should be removed, and the house stand without a foundation, the relative without the correspondent, the accessary without the principal, and the accident without the subject. This is impossible, and therefore it remains that still there abides in the church this power, that by imposition of the hands of fit persons the Holy Ghost is ministered. But this will be further cleared in the next section.

Chapter Three
The holy rite of imposition of hands for the giving the Holy Spirit, or confirmation, was actually continued and practised by all the succeeding ages of the purest and primitive church.

2. Next to the plain words of scripture, the traditive interpretation and practice of the church of god is the best argument in the world for rituals and mystical ministrations; for the tradition is universal, and all the way acknowledged to be derived from scripture. And although in rituals the tradition itself, if it be universal and primitive, as this is, were alone sufficient, and is so esteemed in the baptism of infants, in the priests consecrating the holy eucharist, in public liturgies, in absolution of penitents, the Lord's day, communicating of women, and the like; yet this rite of confirmation being all that, and evidently derived from the practice apostolical, and so often recorded in the New testament, both in the ritual and mysterious part, both in the ceremony and spiritual effect, is a point of as great certainty as it is of usefulness and holy designation.

A.D. 170. Theophilus Antiochenus[1] lived not long after the death of S. John, and he derives the name of Christian, which was first given to the disciples in his city, from this chrism or spiritual unction, this confirmation of baptized persons; ἡμεῖς τούτον εἵνεκεν καλούμεθα Χριστιανοὶ ὅτι χριόμεθα ἔλαιον Θεοῦ, 'we are therefore called Christians because we are anointed with the unction of God.' These words will be best understood by the subsequent testimonies, by which it will appear that confirmation (for reasons hereafter mentioned) was for many ages called chrism or unction. But he adds

---

[1] [Ad Autolyc., lib. i. cap. 12. al. 17.]

the usefulness of it: "for who is there that enters into the world, or that enters into contention or athletic combats, but is anointed with oil?" By which words he intimates the unction anciently used in baptism and in confirmation both; for in the first we have our new birth, in the second we are prepared for spiritual combat.

A.D. 200. Tertullian[2] having spoken of the rites of baptism, proceeds, *Dehinc* (saith he) *manus imponitur, per benedictionem advocans et invitans Spiritum sanctum; tunc ille sanctissimus Spiritus super emundata et benedicta corpora libens a Patre descendit;* 'after baptism the hand is imposed, by blessing calling and inviting the Holy Spirit; then that most Holy Spirit willingly descends from the Father upon the bodies that are cleansed and blessed,' that is, first baptized, then confirmed. And again,[3] *Caro signatur ut anima muniatur; caro manus impositione adumbratur, ut anima Spiritu illuminetur;* 'the flesh is consigned or sealed (that also is one of the known primitive words for confirmation) that the soul may be guarded or defended; and the body is overshadowed by the imposition of hands, that the soul may be enlightened by the Holy Ghost.' Nay further yet, if any man objects that baptism is sufficient, he answers,[4] It is true it is sufficient to them that are to die presently, but it is not enough for them that are still to live and to fight against their spiritual enemies: for "in baptism we do not receive the Holy Ghost" (for although the apostles had been baptized, yet the Holy Ghost was come upon none of them until Jesus was glorified) *sed in aqua emundati, sub angelo Spiritui sancto preparamur,* 'but being cleansed by baptismal water, we are disposed for the Holy Spirit under the hand of the angel' of the church, under the bishop's hand. And a little after he expostulates the article, *Non licebit Deo in suo organo per manus sanctas sublimitatem modulari spiritalem,* 'is it not lawful for God, by an instrument of His own under holy hands to accord the heights and sublimity of the Spirit?' For indeed this is the divine order; and therefore Tertullian[5] reckoning the happiness and excellency of the

---

[2] De baptism, c. 8. [p. 226.]
[3] De resur. carn. bap. viii. [p. 330 C.]
[4] Ubi supra [not. y.] De bapt.
[5] De præscript., cap. xxxvi. [p. 215 B.]

church of Rome at that time, says, "She believes in God, she signs with water, she clothes with the Spirit" (viz. in confirmation) "she feeds with the eucharist, she exhorts to martyrdom; and against this order or institution she receives no man."

A.D. 250. S. Cyprian,[6] in his epistle to Jubaianus, having urged that of the apostles going to Samaria to impose hands on those whom S. Philip had baptized, adds, *Quod nunc quoque apud nos geritur, ut qui in ecclesia baptizantur, per præpositos[7] ecclesiæ offerantur, et per nostram orationem ac manus impositionem Spiritum sanctum consequantur, et signaculo dominico consummentur;* 'which custom is also descended to us, that they who are baptized might be brought by the rulers of the church, and by our prayer and the imposition of hands,' said the martyr bishop, 'may obtain the Holy Ghost, and be consummated with the Lord's signature.' And again,[8] *Ungi necesse est eum qui baptizatus est, &c. Et super eos qui in ecclesia baptizati erant, et ecclesiasticum et legitimum baptismum consecuti fuerant, oratione pro iis habita, et manu imposita, invocaretur et infunderetur Spiritus sanctus*; 'it is necessary that every one who is baptized should receive the unction, that he may be Christ's anointed one, and may have in him the grace of Christ;'. . . 'they who have received lawful and ecclesiastical baptism, it is not necessary they should be baptized again; but that which is wanting must be supplied, viz., that prayer being made for them, and hands imposed, the Holy Ghost be invocated and poured upon them.'

A.D. 200. S. Clement of Alexandria,[9] a man of venerable antiquity and admirable learning, tells that a certain young man was by S. John delivered to the care of a bishop, who having baptized him, *postea vero sigillo domini, tanquam perfecta tutaque ejus custodia,[10] eum obsignavit,* 'afterwards he sealed him with the Lord's signature' (the church word for confirmation) as with a safe and perfect guard.'

---

[6] Epist. lxxiii. [p. 202.]
[7] [al. præpositis.]
[8] Epist. lxx. [p. 190.] et lxxiii. [vid. p. 202.]
[9] Apud Euseb., lib. iii. c. 17. [al. 23.]
[10] Τὸ τέλειον φυλακτήριον.

A.D. 210. Origen[11] in his seventh homily upon Ezekiel, expounding certain mystical words of the prophet, saith, *Oleum est quo vir sanctus ungitur, oleum Christi, oleum sanctæ doctrina: cum ergo accepit aliquis hoc oleum quo ungitur sanctus, id est, scripturam sanctam instituentem quomodo oporteat baptizari in nomine Patris et Filii et Spiritus sancti, et pauca commutans unxerit quempiam, et quodammodo dixerit, Jam non es catechumenus, consecutus es lavacrum secundæ generationis; talis homo accipit oleum Dei, &c.*; 'the unction of Christ, of holy doctrine, is the oil by which the holy man is anointed, having been instructed in the scriptures, and taught how to be baptized; then changing a few things he says to him, Now you are no longer a catechumen, now you are regenerated in baptism: such a man receives the unction of God,' viz. he then is to be confirmed.

S. Dionys, commonly called the Areopagite, in his excellent book of Ecclesiastical Hierarchy,[12] speaks most fully of the holy rite of confirmation or chrism. Having described at large the office and manner of baptizing the catechumens, the trine immersion, the vesting them in white garments, he adds, "Then they bring them again to the bishop, and he consigns him" who had been so baptized θεουργικωτάτῳ μύρῳ, 'with the most divinely operating unction,' and then gives him the most holy eucharist. And afterwards[13] he says, "But even to him who is consecrated in the most holy mystery of regeneration, τοῦ μύρου τελειωτικὴ χρίσις, the perfective unction of chrism gives to him the advent of the Holy Spirit." And this rite of confirmation, then called chrism, from the spiritual unction then effected, and consigned also and signified by the ceremony of anointing externally, which was then the ceremony of the church, he calls it τὴν ἱερὰν τῆς θεογενεσίας τελείωσιν, 'the holy consummation of our baptismal regeneration;' meaning that without this there is something wanting to the baptized persons.

A.D. 260. And this appears fully in that famous censure of Novatus by Cornelius bishop of Rome, reported by Eusebius.[14]

---

[11] [tom. iii. p. 383.]
[12] De eccles. hier., c. ii. [p. 79.]
[13] Cap. iv. [p. 116.]
[14] Lib. vi. hist. eccles. [c. 43.]

Novatus had been baptized in his bed, being very sick and like to die; "but when he recovered, he did not receive those other things which by the rule of the church he ought to have received, *neque Domini sigillo ab episcopo consignatus est*, he was not consigned with the Lord's signature by the hands of the bishop," he was not confirmed; *quo non impetrato, quomodo Spiritum sanctum obtinuisse putandus est*, 'which having not obtained, how can he be supposed to have received the Holy Spirit?' The same also is something more fully related by Nicephorus,[15] but wholly to the same purpose.

A.D. 320. Melchiades,[16] in his epistle to the bishops of Spain, argues excellently about the necessity and usefulness of the holy rite of confirmation. "What does the mystery of confirmation profit me after the mystery of baptism? certainly we did not receive all in our baptism, if after that lavatory we want something of another kind. Let your charity attend. As the military order requires that when the general enters a soldier into his list he does not only mark him but furnishes him with arms for the battle: so in him that is baptized this blessing is his ammunition. You have given (Christ) a soldier, give him also weapons. And what will it profit him if a father gives a great estate to his son if he does not care to provide a tutor for him? Therefore the Holy Spirit is the guardian of our regeneration in Christ, He is the comforter, and He is the defender."

A.D. 370. I have already alleged the plain testimonies of Optatus and S. Cyril[17] in the first section. I add to them the words of S. Gregory Nazianzen[18] speaking of confirmation or the christian signature; *Hoc et viventi tibi maximum est tutamentum; ovis enim que sigillo insignita est non facile patet insidiis, quæ vero signata non est facile a furibus capitur*; 'this signature is your greatest guard while you live; for a sheep when it is marked with the master's sign, is not so soon stolen by thieves, but easily if she be not.' The same manner of speaking is also used by S. Basil,[19] who was himself together with Eubulus confirmed

---

[15] Lib. vi. cap. 3. [tom. i. p. 391.]
[16] [concil. reg., tom. i. p . 698.]
[17] [p. 15 sq. supra.]
[18] Adhort. ad s. lavacrum. [orat. xl. cap. 15. tom. i. p. 701 C.]
[19] [Hom. xiii. tom. ii. p. 117 B.]

by bishop Maximinus; *Quomodo curam geret tanquam ad se pertinentis angelus, quomodo eripiat ex hostibus, si non agnoverit signaculum?* 'How shall the angel know what sheep belong unto his charge, how shall he snatch them from the enemy, if he does not see their mark and signature?' Theodoret also and Theophylact[20] speak the like words; and so far as I can perceive, these and the like sayings are most made use of by the school men to be their warranty for an indelible character imprinted in confirmation: I do not interest myself in the question, but only recite the doctrine of these fathers in behalf of the practice and usefulness of confirmation.

I shall not need to transcribe hither those clear testimonies[21] which are cited from the epistles of S. Clement, Urban the first, Fabianus, and Cornelius; the sum of them is in those plainest words of Urban the first,[22] *Omnes fideles per manus impositionem episcoporum Spiritum sanctum post baptismum accipere debent,* 'all faithful people ought to receive the Holy Spirit by imposition of the bishop's hands after baptism.' Much more to the same purpose is to be read collected by Gratian[23] De consecrate. dist. 4, '*Presbyt.*'; et De consecrate. dist. 5, '*Omnes fideles,*' et ibid. '*Spiritus sanctus.*'

S. Hierome[24] brings in a Luciferian asking, why he that is baptized in the church does not receive the Holy Ghost but by imposition of the bishop's hands. The answer is, *hanc observationem ex scripturæ auctoritate ad sacerdotii honorem descendere,* 'this observation for the honour of the priesthood did descend from the authority of the scriptures;' adding withal, 'it was for the prevention of schisms, and that the safety of the church did depend upon it.' *Erigis ubi scriptum est?* 'If you ask where it is written,' it is answered, *in Actibus apostolorum,* it is written 'in the Acts of the apostles.' But if there were no authority of scripture for it, *totius orbis in hanc partem consensus instar præcepti obtineret,* 'the consent of the whole christian world in this article ought to prevail as a commandment.' But here is a twofold chord, scripture

---

[20] [Ambo] In cap. i. [ver. 13.] ad Ephes.
[21] [cf. p. 31, Jeremy Taylor, *Whole Works,* ed. Heber and Eden, vol. 5.]
[22] [counil. reg., tom. i. p. 293.]
[23] [coll. 2203, 21.]
[24] Dial. adv. Lucifer. [tom. iv. part. 2. col. 294]

and universal tradition; or rather scripture expounded by an universal traditive interpretation. The same observation is made from scripture by S. Chrysostom;[25] the words are very like those now recited from S. Hierome's dialogue, and therefore need not be repeated.

S. Ambrose[26] calls confirmation *spiritale signaculum quod post fontem superest, ut perfectio fiat,* 'a spiritual seal remaining after baptism, that perfection be had.' Œcumenius[27] calls it τελειότητα, 'perfection.' *Lavacro peccata purgantur, chrismate Spiritus sanctus superfunditur; utraque vero ista manu et ore antistitis impetramus,* said Pacianus[28] bishop of Barcinona; 'in baptism our sins are cleansed, in confirmation the Holy Spirit is poured upon us; and both these we obtained by the hands and mouth of the bishop.' And again,[29] *Vestræ plebi unde Spiritus, quam non consignat unctus sacerdos?* The same with that of Cornelius in the case of Novatus before cited.

I shall add no more, lest I overset the article and make it suspicious by too laborious a defence: only after these numerous testimonies of the fathers I think it may be useful to represent that this holy rite of confirmation hath been decreed by many councils.

The council of Eliberis,[30] celebrated in the time of P. Sylvester the first, decreed that whosoever is baptized in his sickness, if he recover, *ad episcopum eum perducat, ut per manus impositionem perfici possit,* 'let him be brought to the bishop, that he may be perfected by the imposition of hands.' To the same purpose is the 77th canon,[31] *Episcopus eos per benedictionem perficere debebit,* 'the bishop must perfect those' whom the minister baptized, 'by his benediction.'

The council of Laodicea[32] decreed ὅτι δεῖ τοὺς φωτιζομένους μετὰ τὸ βάπτισμα χρίεσθαι χρίσματι ἐπουρανίῳ, καὶ μετόχους εἶναι τῆς βασιλείας τοῦ Χριστοῦ, 'all that are baptized must be anointed with the celestial unction, and [so] be partakers of the kingdom of Christ.'

---

[25] Homil. xviii. in Act. [tom. ix. p. 146 D.]
[26] Lib. iii. De sacram. c. 2. [tom. ii. col. 363 E.]
[27] In Hebr. vi. [vid. in ver. 2.]
[28] [De bapt.—Magn. bibl. vett. patr., tom. iv. p. 247.]
[29] Lib. iii. cont. Novat. [ibid. p. 239 C.]
[30] Can. 38. [tom. i. col. 254.]
[31] [col. 258.]
[32] [can. 28. tom. i. col. 789.]

All that are so (that is, are confirmed, for this celestial unction is done "by holy prayers and the invocation of the Holy Spirit," so Zonaras[33] upon this canon; all such who have this unction) shall reign with Christ, unless by their wickedness they preclude their own possessions. This canon was put into the code of the catholic church, and makes the 152nd canon.

The council of Orleans[34] affirms expressly that he who is baptized cannot be a Christian (meaning according to the usual style of the church, a full and perfect Christian) *nisi confirmatione episcopali fuerit chrismatus*, 'unless he have the unction of episcopal confirmation.'

But when the church had long disputed concerning the re-baptizing of heretics, and made canons for and against it according as the heresies were, and all agreed that if the first baptism had been once good it could never be repeated; yet they thought it fit that such persons should be confirmed by the bishop, all supposing confirmation to be the perfection and consummation of the less perfect baptism. Thus the first council of Arles[35] decreed concerning the Arians, that if they had been baptized in the name of the Father, Son, and Holy Ghost, they should not be re-baptized, *Manus tantum eis impo natur ut accipiant Spiritum sanctum*; that is, 'let them be confirmed, let there be imposition of hands that they may receive the Holy Ghost.' The same is decreed by the second council of Arles[36] in the case of the Bonosiaci. But I also find it in a greater record, in the general council of Constantinople,[37] where heretics are commanded upon their conversion to be received *secundum constitutum officium*. There was an office appointed for it, and it is in the Greeks' Euchologion;[38] *Sigillatos, primo scil. unctos unguento chrismatis, &c.—Et*

---

[33] [Bevereg. Synod., tom. i. p. 475.]
[34] Habetur apud Gratian. de Consecrat. dist. v. cap. 'Ut jejuni.' [sc. cap. vi. col. 2224.]
[35] Cap. 8. [tom. i. col. 265.]
[36] Can. 17. [tom. ii. col. 774.]
[37] Can 7. [tom. i. col. 812.]
[38] [Goar, p. 880.]

signantes eos dicimus, Sigillum doni Spiritus sancti. It is the form of confirmation used to this day in the Greek church.

So many fathers testifying the practice of the church and teaching this doctrine, and so many more fathers as were assembled in six councils all giving witness to this holy rite, and that in pursuance also of scripture, are too great a cloud of witnesses to be despised by any man that calls himself a Christian.

Chapter Four
The bishops were always, and the only ministers of confirmation.

Saint Chrysostom[1] asking the reason why the Samaritans, who were baptized by Philip, could not from him and by his ministry receive the Holy Ghost, answers, "Perhaps this was done for the honour of the apostles," to distinguish the supereminent dignity which they bore in the church from all inferior ministrations: but this answer not satisfying, he adds, *Hoc donum non habebat, erat enim ex septem illis, id quod magis videtur dicendum: unde (mea sententia) hic Philippus unus ex septem erat, secundus a Stephano; ideo et baptizans Spiritum sanctum non dabat, neque enim facultatem habebat, hoc enim donum solorum apostolorum erat*; 'this gift they had not who baptized the Samaritans, which thing is rather to be said than the other: for Philip was one of the seven, and in my opinion next to S. Stephen; therefore though he baptized yet he gave not the Holy Ghost, for he had no power so to do, for this gift was proper only to the apostles.' *Nam virtutem quidem acceperant (diaconi) faciendi signa, non autem dandi aliis Spiritum sanctum; igitur hoc erat in apostolis singulare, unde et præcipuos, et non alios, videmus hoc facere*; 'the ministers that baptized had a power of doing signs and working miracles, but not of giving the Holy Spirit; therefore this gift was peculiar to the apostles, whence it comes to pass that we see the chiefs[2] in the church, and no other, to do this.'

---

[1] Homil. xviii. in Acta. [tom. ix. p. 146 D.]
[2] τοὺς κορυφαίους.

S. Dionys[3] says, χρεία τοῦ ἀρχιερέως ἔσται, 'there is need of a bishop' to confirm the baptized, αὐτὴ γὰρ ἦν ἡ ἀρχαία συνήθεια, 'for this was the ancient custom' of the church. And this was wont to be done by the bishops for conservation of unity in the church of Christ, said S. Ambrose;[4] *a solis episcopis*, 'by bishops only,' said S. Austin;[5] "for the bishops succeeded in the place and ordinary office of the apostles," said S. Hierome.[6] And therefore in his dialogue against the Luciferians[7] it is said that "this observation for the honour of the priesthood did descend that the bishops only might by imposition of hands confer the Holy Ghost; that it comes from scripture, that it is written in the Acts of the apostles, that it is done for the prevention of schisms, that the safety of the church depends upon it."

But the words of P. Innocentius the first[8] in his first epistle and third chapter, and published in the first tome of the councils, are very full to this particular. *De consignandis infantibus, manifestum est non ab alio quam ab episcopo fieri licere; nam presbyteri, licet sint sacerdotes, pontificatus tamen apicem non habent: hæc autem pontificibus solis deberi, ut vel consignent, vel Paracletum spiritum tradant, non solum consuetudo ecclesiastica demonstrat, verum et illa lectio Actuum apostolorum, quæ asserit Petrum et Joannem esse directos qui jam baptizatis traderent Spiritum sanctum*; 'concerning confirmation of infants, it is manifest it is not lawful to be done by any other than by the bishop; for although the presbyters be priests, yet they have not the summity of episcopacy; but that these things are only due to bishops is not only demonstrated by the custom of the church, but by that of the Acts of the apostles, where Peter and John were sent to minister the Holy Ghost to them that were baptized.' Optatus[9] proves Macarius to be no bishop, because he was not conversant in the episcopal office, and imposed hands on none that were baptized. *Hoc unum a majoribus fit, id est, a summis pontificibus, quod*

---

[3] Cap. v. Eccles. hier. [leg. Pachymeres, p. 72, ad calc. opp. S. Dionys.—vid. p. 123., Jeremy Taylor, *Whole Works*, ed. Heber and Eden, vol. 5.]
[4] In Hebr. vi. [? vid. p. 41, not. x, Taylor, *Whole Works*, ed. Heber and Eden, vol. 5.]
[5] Qu. 44. in N.T. [leg. 42. al. 93. tom. iii. append. col. 84.]
[6] [p. 41, Taylor, *Whole Works*, ed. Heber and Eden, vol. 5.]
[7] [Chap. 3., not. 24., supra.]
[8] [council. reg., tom. i. p. 7.]
[9] Contr. Parmen., lib. vii. [cap. 6.]

a minoribus perfici non potest, said P. Melchiades,[10] 'this (of confirmation) is only done by the greater ministers, that is, by the bishops, and cannot be done by the lesser.' This was the constant practice and doctrine of the primitive church, and derived from the practice and tradition of the apostles, and recorded in their acts written by S. Luke. For this is our great rule in this case, what they did in rituals and consigned to posterity is our example and our warranty: we see it done thus, and by these men, and by no others and no otherwise, and we have no other authority, and we have no reason to go another way. The ἄνδρες ἡγούμενοι in S. Luke, the κορυφαῖοι in S. Chrysostom, the πρόεδος in Philo, and the πρεσβύτατος, the chief governor in ecclesiasticals, his office is τὰ μὴ γνώριμα ἐν τοῖς βίβλοις ἀναδιδάσκειν, 'to teach such things as are not set down in books;' their practice is a sermon, their example in these things must be our rule, or else we must walk irregularly, and have no rule but chance and humour, empire and usurpation; and therefore much rather when it is recorded in holy writ must this observation be esteemed sacred and inviolable.

But how if a bishop be not to be had or not ready? S. Ambrose[11] is pretended to have answered, *Apud Ægyptum presbyteri consignant, si præsens non sit episcopus*, 'a presbyter may consign if the bishop be not present;' and Amalarius[12] affirms, *Sylvestrum papam, prævidentem quantum periculosum iter arriperet qui sine confirmatione maneret, quantum potuit subvenisse, et propter absentiam episcoporum, necessitate addidisse, ut a presbytero ungerentur*, 'that pope Sylvester, foreseeing how dangerous a journey he takes who abides without confirmation, brought remedy as far as he could, and commanded that in the absence of bishops they should be anointed by the priest:' and therefore it is by some supposed that *Factum valet, fieri non debuit*, 'the thing ought not to be done but in the proper and appointed way, but when it is done it is

---

[10] Epist. ad Episc. Hispan. [cap. 2. p. 698.]
    Voluit Deus dona illa admiranda non contingere baptizatis nisi per manus apostolorum, ut auctoritatem testibus suis conciliaret quam maximam; quod ipsum simul ad retinendam ecclesiæ unitatem pertinebat. —Grotius. [in Act. viii. 15.]
[11] In Eph. iv. [ver. 12, tom. ii. append. col. 241 F.]
[12] De. office. Eccles. [lib. i.] cap. 27.

valid;' just as in the case of baptism by a layman or woman. Nay, though some canons say it is *actio irrita*, the act is null, yet for this there is a *salvo* pretended; for sometimes an action is said to be *irrita* in law, which yet nevertheless is of secret and permanent value, and ought not to be done again. Thus if a priest be promoted by simony, it is said,[13] *sacerdos non est, sed inaniter tantum dicitur*, 'he is but vainly called a priest, for he is no priest.' So Sixtus the second[14] said that if a bishop ordain in another's diocese the ordination is void; and in the law[15] it is said that if a bishop be consecrated without his clergy and the congregation, the consecration is null; and yet these later and fiercer constitutions do not determine concerning the natural event of things, but of the legal and canonical approbation.

To these things I answer[16] that S. Ambrose his saying that in Egypt the presbyters consign in the bishop's absence, does not prove that they ever did confirm or impose hands on the baptized for the ministry of the Holy Spirit; because that very passage being related by S. Austin,[17] the more general word of 'consign' is rendered by the plainer and more particular *consecrant*, 'they consecrate,' meaning the blessed eucharist; which was not permitted primitively to a simple priest to do in the bishop's absence without leave, only in Egypt it seems they had a general leave, and the bishop's absence was an interpretative consent. But besides this, *consignant* is best interpreted by the practice of the church, of which I shall presently give an account; they might in the absence of the bishop consign with oil upon the top of the head, but not in the forehead, much less impose hands, or confirm, or minister the Holy Spirit: for the case was this;—

It was very early in the church that to represent the grace which was ministered in confirmation, the unction from above, they used oil and balsam, and so constantly used this in their confirmations that

---

[13] [Decret. caus.] i. qu. 1. cap. 'Qui vult.' [leg. 'Quicumque studet.'] 1 et 2. [col. 533.]
[14] Epist. ii. de episc. ordin. [council. reg., tom. i. p. 533.]
[15] [Decret.] c. i. qu. 2. [leg. 3.] c. 'Ex multis.' [col. 625.]—Clement. de elect. cap. 'In plerisque.' [ad calc. decret. Bonifac. col. 45.]
[16] [He might now have answered that the commentary is considered spurious. Taylor himself elsewhere speaks of the passage with suspicion; see p. 126. Taylor, *Whole Works*, ed. Heber and Eden, vol. 5.]
[17] Qu. V. et N.T. qu. 101. [tom. iii. append. col. 93.]

from the ceremony it had the appellation; *sacramentum chrismatis* S. Austin[18] calls it; ἐν μύρῳ τελείωσις, so Dionysius.[19] Now because at the baptism of the adult Christians and (by imitation of that) of infants, confirmation and baptism were usually ministered at the same time; the unction was not only used to persons newly baptized, but another unction was added as a ceremony in baptism itself, and was used immediately before baptism; and the oil was put on the top of the head, and three times was the party signed. So it was then, as we find in the Ecclesiastical Hierarchy. But besides this unction with oil in baptismal preparations, and pouring oil into the baptismal water, we find another unction after the baptism was finished. "For they bring the baptized person again to the bishop," saith S. Dionys,[20] "who signing the man with hallowed chrism, gives him the holy eucharist." This they called χρίσιν τελειωτικὴν, 'the perfective or consummating unction:' this was that which was used when the bishop confirmed the baptized person: "for to him who is initiated by the most holy initiation of the divine generation " (that is, "to him who hath been baptized," saith Pachymeres[21] the paraphrast of Dionysius) "the perfective unction of chrism gives the gift of the Holy Ghost." This is that which the Laodicean council[22] calls χρίεσθαι μετὰ τὸ βάπτισμα, 'to be anointed after baptism.' Both these unctions were intimated by Theophilus Antiochenus,[23] Τίς δὲ ἄνθρωπος εἰσελθὼν εἰς τόνδε τὸν βίον, ἢ ἀθλῶν, οὐ χρίεται ἐλαίῳ; 'every man that is born into the world, and every man that is a champion, is anointed with oil;' that to baptism, this alluding to confirmation.

Now this chrism was frequently ministered immediately after baptism, in the cities where the bishop was present; but in villages and little towns where the bishop was not present it could not be, but bishops were forced at their opportunities to go abroad and perfect what was wanting, as it was in the example of Peter and John to the

---

[18] Lib. ii. cont. liter. Petiliani, c. 104.
[19] [p. 10 supra.]
[20] Eccles. hier., cap. 2. [p. 85.]
[21] [p. 54.—vid. p. 123 Taylor, *Whole Works,* ed. Heber and Eden, vol. 5.]
[22] Can. 48. [tom. i. col. 789.]
[23] [vid. Chap. 3, not. 1, supra.]

Samaritans. *Non quidem abnuo hanc esse ecclesiarum consuetudinem, et ad eos qui longe in minoribus urbibus per presbyteros et diaconos baptizati sunt, episcopus ad invocationem sancti Spiritus manum impositurus excurrat;*[24] 'it is the custom of the church, that when persons are in lesser cities baptized by priests and deacons, the bishop uses to travel far, that he may lay hands on them for the invocation of the Holy Spirit." But because this could not always be done, and because many baptized persons died before such an opportunity could be had; the church took up a custom, that the bishop should consecrate the chrism and send it to the villages and little cities distant from the metropolis, and that the priests should anoint the baptized with it. But still they kept this part of it sacred and peculiar to the bishop; first, that no chrism should be used but what the bishop consecrated; secondly, that the priests should anoint the head of the baptized, but at no hand the forehead, for that was still reserved for the bishop to do when he confirmed them. And this is evident in the epistle of P. Innocent[25] the first, above quoted. *Nam presbyteris, seu extra episcopum seu prasente episcopo baptizant, chrismate baptizatos ungere licet, sed quod ab episcopo fuerit consecratum; non tamen frontem ex eodem oleo signare, quod solis debetur episcopis cum tradunt Spiritum paracletum.* Now this the bishops did, not only to satisfy the desire of the baptized, but by this ceremony to excite the *votum confirmationis*, that they who could not actually be confirmed, might at least have it *in voto*, 'in desire,' and in ecclesiastical representation. This, as some think, was first introduced by pope Sylvester: and this is the consignation which the priests of Egypt used in the absence of the bishop; and this became afterward the practice in other churches.

But this was no part of the holy rite of confirmation, but a ceremony annexed to it ordinarily; from thence transmitted to baptism, first by imitation, afterwards by way of supply and in defect of the opportunities of confirmation episcopal. And therefore we find in the first Arausican council,[26] in the time of Leo the first and

---

[24] S. Hieron. adv. Lucifer. ante med. [tom. iv. part. 2. col. 295.]
[25] [cap. 3.—Concil. reg., tom. i. p. 7.]
[26] [can. 2. tom. i. col. 1784.]

Theodosius junior, it was decreed that in baptism every one should receive chrism; *De eo autem qui in baptismate, quacunque necessitate faciente, chrismatus non fuerit, in confirmatione sacerdos commonebitur,* 'if the baptized by any intervening accident or necessity was not anointed, the bishop should be advertised of it in confirmation;' meaning that then it must be done. For the chrism was but a ceremony annexed, no part of either rite essential to it; but yet they thought it necessary by reason of some opinions then prevailing in the church. But here the rites themselves are clearly distinguished; and this of confirmation was never permitted to mere presbyters. Innocentius the third,[27] a great canonist and of great authority, gives a full evidence in this particular. *Per frontis chrismationem manus impositio designatur, . .quia*[28] *per eam Spiritus sanctus ad augmentum datur et robur; unde cum cæteras unctiones simplex sacerdos vel presbyter valeat exhibere, hanc non nisi summus sacerdos, id est, episcopus debet conferre*; 'by anointing of the forehead the imposition of hands is designed, because by that the Holy Ghost is given for increase and strength; therefore when a single priest may give the other unctions, yet this cannot be done but by the chief priest, that is, the bishop.' And therefore to the question what shall be done if a bishop may not be had? the same Innocentius answers, "It is safer and without danger wholly to omit it than to have it rashly and without authority ministered by any other, *cum umbra quadam ostendatur in opere, veritas autem non subeat in effectu*, for it is a mere shadow without truth or real effect when any one else does it but the person whom God hath appointed to this ministration." And no approved man of the church did ever say the contrary, till Richard primate of Ardmagh[29] commenced a new opinion, from whence (Thomas of Walden[30] says that) Wiclef borrowed his doctrine to trouble the church in this particular.

What the doctrine of the ancient church was in the purest times I have already (I hope) sufficiently declared; what it was afterwards when the ceremony of chrism was as much remarked as the rite to

---

[27] [Decret. constit., lib. i. c. 83. tom. ii. p. 627.]
[28] [...'designatur, quæ alio nominee dicitur confirmation, quia'. . . &c.]
[29] [Chap. 1., not. 3., supra.]
[30] [De sacram. confirm.,—opp. tom. ii. fol. 187 b sqq.—fol. Venet. 1571.]

which it ministered, we find fully declared by Rabanus Maurus.[31] *Signatur baptizatus cum chrismate per sacerdotem in capitis summitate, per pontificem vero in fronte; ut priori unctione significetur Spiritus sancti super ipsum descensio ad habitationem Deo consecrandam; in secunda quoque, ut ejus Spiritus sancti septiformis gratia, cum omni plenitudine sanctitatis et scientiæ et virtutis, venire in hominem declaretur: tunc enim ipse Spiritus sanctus post mundata et benedicta corpora atque animas libens a Patre descendit, ut vas suum sua visitatione sanctificet et illustret; et nunc in hominem ad hoc venit, ut signaculum fidei quod in fronte suscepit, faciat eum donis cælestibus repletum, et sua gratia confortatum, intrepide et audacter coram regibus et potestatibus hujus sæculi portare, ac nomen Christi libera voce prædicare*; 'in baptism the baptized was anointed on the top of the head, in confirmation on the forehead: by that was signified that the Holy Ghost was preparing a habitation for Himself; by this was declared the descent of the Holy Spirit, with His seven-fold gifts, with all fulness of knowledge and spiritual understanding.' These things were signified by the appendent ceremony; but the rites were ever distinguished, and did not only signify and declare but effect these graces by the ministry of prayer and imposition of hands.

The ceremony the church instituted and used as she pleased, and gave in what circumstances they would choose; and new propositions entered, and customs changed, and deputations were made, and the bishops in whom by Christ was placed the fulness of ecclesiastical power concredited to the priests and deacons so much as their occasions and necessities permitted: and because in those ages and places where the external ceremony was regarded (it may be) more than the inward mystery or the rite of divine appointment, they were apt to believe that the chrism or exterior unction delegated to the priests' ministry after the episcopal consecration of it, might supply the want of episcopal confirmation; it came to pass that new opinions were entertained, and the Regulars, the Friars and the Jesuits, who were always too little friends to the episcopal power, from which they would fain have been wholly exempted, publicly taught (in England especially) that chrism ministered by them with

---

[31] De instit. cleric., lib. i. c. 30. [tom. vi. p. 10.]

leave from the pope did do all that which ordinarily was to be done in episcopal confirmation. For as Tertullian complained in his time, *quibus fuit proposi tum aliter docendi, eos necessitas coegit aliter disponendi instrumenta doctrinæ*; 'they who had purposes of teaching new doctrines were constrained otherwise to dispose of the instruments and rituals appertaining to their doctrines.' These men, to serve ends, destroyed the article, and overthrew the ancient discipline and unity of the primitive church; but they were justly censured by the theological faculty at Paris, and the censure well defended by Hallier, one of the doctors of the Sorbon, whither I refer the reader that is curious in little things.

But for the main; it was ever called *confirmatio episcopalis, et impositio manuum episcoporum*; which our English word well expresses and perfectly retains the use; we know it by the common name of 'bishopping' of children. I shall no further insist upon it, only I shall observe that there is a vain distinction brought into the schools and glosses of the canon law, of a minister ordinary and extraordinary; all allowing that the bishop is appointed the ordinary minister of confirmation, but they would fain innovate and pretend that in some cases others may be ministers extraordinary. This device is of infinite danger, to the destruction of the whole sacred order of the ministry, and disparks the inclosures, and lays all in common, and makes men supreme controllers of the orders of God, and relies upon a false principle, for in true divinity and by the economy of the Spirit of God, there can be no minister of any divine ordinance but he that is of divine appointment, there can be none but the ordinary minister. I do not say that God is tied to this way; He cannot be tied but by Himself: and therefore Christ gave a special commission to Ananias to baptize and to confirm S. Paul, and He gave the Spirit to Cornelius even before he was baptized, and He ordained S. Paul to be an apostle without the ministry of man. But this I say, that though God can make ministers extraordinary, yet man cannot, and they that go about to do so usurp the power of Christ, and snatch from His hand what He never intended to part with. The apostles admitted others into a part of their care and of their power, but when they intended to employ them in any ministry, they gave them so much of their order as would enable them; but a person of lower order could never be deputed minister of actions appropriate to the higher: which is the case of confirmation, by the practice and tradition of the apostles and by the universal practice and doctrine of the primitive catholic church, by which bishops only, the successors of the apostles, were alone the ministers of confirmation: and therefore if any man else usurp it, let them answer it; they do hurt indeed to themselves, but no benefit to others, to whom they minister shadows instead of substances.

Chapter Five
The whole procedure or ritual of confirmation is by prayer and imposition of hands.

The heart and the eye are lift up to God to bring blessings from Him, and so is the hand too; but this also falls upon the people and rests there to apply the descending blessing to the proper and prepared suscipient. God governed the people of Israel by the hand of Moses and Aaron,

>   ——et calidæ fecere silentia turbæ
> Majestate manus:[1]

and both under Moses and under Christ, whenever the president of religion did bless the people, he lifted up his hand over the congregation; and when he blessed a single person he laid his hand upon him. This was the rite used by Jacob and the patriarchs, by kings and prophets, by all the eminently religious in the synagogue, and by Christ himself when He blessed the children which were brought to Him, and by the apostles when they blessed and confirmed the baptized converts; and whom else can the church follow? The apostles did so to the Christians of Samaria, to them of Ephesus; and S. Paul describes this whole mystery by the ritual part of it, calling it the foundation of the imposition of hands.[2] It is the solemnity of blessing, and the solemnity and application of paternal prayer. Τίνι

---

[1] [Pers. sat. iv. 7.]
[2] [Heb. vi. 2.]

γὰρ ἐπιτίθησι χεῖρα; τίνα δὲ εὐλογήσει; said Clement of Alexandria,[3] 'Upon whom shall he lay his lands? whom shall he bless?' *Quid enim aliud est impositio manuum, nisi oratio super hominem?* said S. Austin,[4] 'The bishop's laying his hands on the people, what is it but the solemnity of prayer for them?' that is, a prayer made by those sacred persons who by Christ are appointed to pray for them, and to bless in His name: and so indeed are all the ministries of the church, baptism, consecration of the B. eucharist, absolution, ordination, visitation of the sick; they are all in *genere orationis*, they are nothing but solemn and appointed prayer by an intrusted and a gracious person, specificated by a proper order to the end of the blessing then designed. And therefore when S. James commanded that the sick persons should send for the elders of the church, he adds, And let them 'pray over' them, that is, 'lay their hands on' the sick, and 'pray for them; that is 'praying over them': it is *adumbratio dextræ*, as Tertullian[5] calls it, the right hand of him that ministers over-shadows the person for whom the solemn prayer is to be made.

This is the office of the rulers of the church; for they in the divine eutaxy are made your superiors: they are indeed "your servants for Jesus' sake," but they are "over you in the Lord," and therefore are from the Lord appointed to bless the people; for "without contradiction," saith the apostle,[6] "the less is blessed of the greater;" that is, God hath appointed the superiors in religion to be the great ministers of prayer, He hath made them the gracious persons, them He will hear, those He hath commanded to convey your needs to God, and God's blessings to you, and to ask a blessing is to desire them to pray for you; them, I say, "whom God most respecteth for their piety and zeal that way, or else regardeth for that their place and calling bindeth them above others to do this duty, such as are[7] natural and spiritual fathers."[8]

---

[3] Pædag., lib. iii. c. 11. [p. 291.]
[4] [De bapt. contr. Donat. iii. 16.]
[5] [vid. De resurrect. carn., c. viii.]
[6] [Heb. vii. 7.]
[7] [leg. 'as it doth.']
[8] Hooker, Eccl. pol., lib. v. [ch. 66.]

It is easy for profane persons to deride these things, as they do all religion which is not conveyed to them by sense or natural demonstrations; but the economy of the Spirit and the things of God are spiritually discerned: "the Spirit bloweth where it listeth, and no man knows whence it comes, and whither it goes;" and the operations are discerned by faith, and received by love and by obedience. *Date mihi christianum, et intelligit quod dico*; 'none but true Christians understand and feel these things.' But of this we are sure, that in all the times of Moses' law, while the synagogue was standing, and in all the days of christianity, so long as men loved religion and walked in the Spirit and minded the affairs of their souls, to have the prayers and the blessing of the fathers of the synagogue and the fathers of the church was esteemed no small part of their religion, and so they went to heaven. But that which I intend to say is this, that prayer and imposition of hands was the whole procedure in the christian rites; and because this ministry was most signally performed by this ceremony, and was also by S. Paul called and noted by the name of the ceremony, 'Imposition of hands,' this name was retained in the christian church, and this manner of ministering confirmation was all that was in the commandment or institution.

But because in confirmation we receive the unction from above, that is, then we are most signally 'made kings and priests unto God, to offer up spiritual sacrifices,' and to enable us to 'seek the kingdom of God and the righteousness of it,' and that the giving of the Holy Spirit is in scripture called the unction from above; the church of God in early ages made use of this allegory, and passed it into an external ceremony and representation of the mystery, to signify the inward grace.

> Post inscripta oleo frontis signacula, per quæ
> Unguentum regale datum est, et chrisma perenne;[9]

'we are consigned on the forehead with oil, and a royal unction and an eternal chrism is given to us;' so Prudentius gives testimony of the ministry of confirmation in his time, 400 A.D. Τοῦτο φυλάξατε

---

[9] Prudent. in ψυχομαχίᾳ, lin. 361. [tom. ii. p. 619.]

ἄσπιλον, πάντων γάρ ἐστι[10] τοῦτο διδακτικὸν, καθὼς ἀρτίως ἠκούσατε τοῦ μακαρίου Ἰωάννου λέγαντος καὶ πολλὰ περὶ τούτου χρίσματος φιλοσοφοῦντος, said S. Cyril;[11] 'preserve this unction pure and spotless, for it teaches you all things, as you have heard the blessed S. John speaking and philosophizing many things of this holy chrism.' Upon this account the H. fathers used to bless and consecrate oil and balsam, that by an external signature they might signify the inward unction effected in confirmation: μύρον τοῦτο οὐκ ἔστι ψιλὸν, οὐδ᾽ ὡς ἄν τις εἴποι κοινὸν μετ᾽ ἐπίκλησιν, ἀλλὰ Χριστοῦ χάρισμα καὶ Πνεύματος ἁγίου παρουμίας, τῆς αὐτοῦ θεότητος ἐνεργητικὸν γινόμενον, 'this chrism is not simple or common when it is blessed, but the gift of Christ and the presence of His H. spirit, as it were effecting the divinity itself;' the body is indeed anointed with visible ointment, but is also sanctified by the holy and quickening Spirit: so S. Cyril.[12] I find in him and in some late synods[13] other pretty significations and allusions made by this ceremony of chrisms. *Nos autem pro igne visibili qui die pentecostes super apostolos apparuit, oleum sanctum, materiam nempe ignis, ex apostolorum traditione ad confirmandum adhibemus*, 'this using of oil was instead of the baptism with fire which Christ baptized His apostles with in Pentecost, and oil being the most proper matter of fire is therefore used in confirmation.'

That this was the ancient ceremony is without doubt, and that the church had power to do so hath no question; and I add, it was not unreasonable, for if ever the scripture expresses the mysteriousness of a grace conferred by an exterior ministry (as this is by imposition of hands) and represents it besides in the expression and analogy of any sensible thing, that expression drawn into a ceremony will not improperly signify the grace, since the Holy Ghost did choose that for His own expression and representment. In baptism we are said to be buried with Christ; the church does according to the analogy of that expression when she immerges the

---

[10] [leg. ἔσται.]
[11] Catech. [xxii.] mystag. iii. [cap. 7. p. 318 A.]
[12] [Ibid., cap. 3. p. 317.]
[13] Synodus Bituricensis, apud Bochell., lib. i. [leg. ii.] decret. eccl. Gal. tit. g. [cap. 10.]

catechumen in the font, for then she represents the same thing which the Holy Ghost would have to be represented in that sacrament. The church did but the same thing when she used chrism in this ministration. This I speak in justification of that ancient practice; but because there was no command for it,—λόγος γεγραμμένος οὐκ ἔστι, said S. Basil,[14] 'concerning chrism there is no written word,' that is, of the ceremony there is not, he said it not of the whole rite of confirmation,—therefore though to this we are all bound, yet as to the anointing the church is at liberty, and hath with sufficient authority omitted it in our ministrations.

In the liturgy of king Edward the sixth the bishops used the sign of the cross upon the foreheads of them that were to be confirmed. I do not find it since forbidden or revoked by any expression or intimation, saving only that it is omitted in our later offices; and therefore it may seem to be permitted to the discretion of the bishops, but yet not to be used unless where it may be for edification, and where it may be by the consent of the church, at least by interpretation; concerning which I have nothing else to interpose, but that neither this nor any thing else which is not of the nature and institution of the rite, ought to be done by private authority, nor ever at all but according to the apostle's rule, εὐσχημόνως καὶ κατὰ τάξιν· whatsoever is decent, and whatsoever is according to order, that is to be done, and nothing else: for prayer and imposition of hands for the invocating and giving the Holy Spirit is all that is in the foundation and institution.

---

[14] Lib. de Spir. S., cap. 17. [leg. 27. tom. iii. p. 55 A.]

Chapter Six
Many great graces and blessings are consequent to the worthy reception and due ministry of confirmation.

It is of itself enough, when it is fully understood, what is said in the Acts of the apostles at the first ministration of this rite, "they received the Holy Ghost;" that is, according to the expression of our blessed Saviour himself to the apostles when He commanded them in Jerusalem to expect the verification of His glorious promise, "they were endued with virtue from on high;" that is, with strength to perform their duty: which although it is not to be understood exclusively to the other rites and ministries of the church of divine appointment, yet it is properly and most signally true, and as it were in some sense appropriate to this. For as Aquinas[1] well discourses, the grace of Christ is not tied to the sacraments; but even this spiritual strength and virtue from on high can be had without confirmation, as without baptism remission of sins may be had: and yet we 'believe one baptism for the remission of sins,' and one confirmation for the obtaining this virtue from on high, this strength of the Spirit. But it is so appropriate to it by promise and peculiarity of ministration, that as without the desire of baptism our sins are not pardoned, so without at least the desire of confirmation we cannot receive this virtue from on high, which is appointed to descend in the ministry of the Spirit. It is true the ministry of the holy eucharist is greatly effective to this purpose; and therefore in the ages of martyrs the bishops were careful to give the people the holy communion frequently, *ut quos tutos esse*

---

[1] Part. iii. qu. 72. [art. 6. 'ad prim.']

contra adversarium volebant munimento dominicæ saturitatis armarent, as S. Cyprian[2] with his colleagues wrote to Cornelius, 'that those whom they would have to be safe against the contentions of their adversaries, they should arm them with the guards and defences of the Lord's fulness.' But it is to be remembered that the Lord's supper is for the more perfect Christians, and it is for the increase of the graces received formerly, and therefore it is for remission of sins, and yet is no prejudice to the necessity of baptism, whose proper work is remission of sins; and therefore neither does it make confirmation unnecessary: for it renews the work of both the precedent rites, and repairs the breaches, and adds new energy, and proceeds in the same dispensations, and is renewed often, whereas the others are but once.

Excellent therefore are the words of John Gerson,[3] the famous chancellor of Paris, to this purpose. "It may be said that in one way of speaking confirmation is necessary, and in another it is not. Confirmation is not necessary as baptism and repentance, for without these salvation cannot be had; this necessity is absolute. But there is a conditional necessity: thus if a man would not become weak it is necessary that he eat his meat well: and so confirmation is necessary that the spiritual life and the health gotten in baptism may be preserved in strength against our spiritual enemies; for this is given for strength. Hence is that saying of Hugo de S. Victore, 'What does it profit that thou art raised up by baptism if thou art not able to stand by confirmation?' Not that baptism is not of value unto salvation without confirmation, but because he who is not confirmed will easily fall and too readily perish." The Spirit of God comes which way He pleases, but we are tied to use His own economy and expect the blessings appointed by His own ministries: and because to prayer is promised we shall receive whatever we ask, we may as well omit the receiving the holy eucharist, pretending that prayer alone will procure the blessings expected in the other, as well, I say, as omit confirmation, because we hope to be strengthened and receive virtue

---

[2] Epist. liv. [al. lvii. p. 117.]
[3] In opusc. aur. de Confirmat. [De septem sacramentis, art. De confirmation, tom. ii. col. 78.]

from on high by the use of the supper of the Lord. Let us use all the ministries of grace in their season; for "we know not which shall prosper, this or that, or whether they shall be both alike good;"[4] this only we know, that the ministries which God appoints are the proper seasons and opportunities of grace.

This power from on high, which is the proper blessing of confirmation, was expressed not only in speaking with tongues and doing miracles, for much of this they had before they received the Holy Ghost, but it was effected in spiritual and internal strengths; they were not only enabled for the service of the church, but were indued with courage and wisdom and christian fortitude and boldness to confess the faith of Christ crucified, and unity of heart and mind, singleness of heart, and joy in God. When it was for the edification of the church, miracles were done in confirmations; and S. Bernard,[5] in the life of S. Malachias, tells that S. Malchus, bishop of Lismore in Ireland, confirmed a lunatic child, and at the same time cured him: but such things as these are extra-regular and contingent: this which we speak of is a regular ministry and must have a regular effect.

S. Austin[6] said that the Holy Spirit in confirmation was given *ad dilatanda ecclesiæ primordia*, 'for the propagating christianity in the beginnings of the church.' S. Hierome[7] says, it was *propter honorem sacerdotii*, 'for the honour of the priesthood.' S. Ambrose[8] says, it was *ad confirmationem unitatis in ecclesia Christi*, 'for the confirmation of unity in the church of Christ.' And they all say true; but the first was by the miraculous consignations which did accompany this ministry, and the other two were by reason that the mysteries were τὰ προτελεσθέντα ὑπὸ τοῦ ἐπισκόπου, they were 'appropriated to the ministry of the bishop,' who is *caput unitatis*, the head, the last resort, the firmament of unity in the church. These effects were regular indeed, but they were incident and accidental: there are effects yet more proper and of greater excellency.

---

[4] [Eccles. xi. 6.]
[5] [col. 1932.]
[6] [De bapt. contra Donat., lib. iii. cap. 16. tom. ix. col. 116 F.]
[7] [vid. p. 124, not. k, Taylor, *Whole Works,* ed. Heber and Eden, vol. 5.]
[8] [Chap. 4, not. 4, supra.]

Now if we will understand in general what excellent fruits are consequent to this dispensation, we may best receive the notice of them from the fountain itself, our blessed Saviour. "He that believes, out of his belly, as the scripture saith, shall flow rivers of living waters. But this He spake of the Spirit, which they that believe on Him should receive."[9] This is evidently spoken of the Spirit which came down in Pentecost, which was promised to all that should believe in Christ, and which the apostles ministered by imposition of hands, the Holy Ghost himself being the expositor; and it can signify no less but that a spring of life should be put into the heart of the confirmed, to water the plants of God; that they should become trees, not only planted by the water side (for so it was in David's time and in all the ministry of the Old testament) but having a river of living water within them to make them fruitful of good works, and bringing their fruit in due season, fruits worthy of amendment of life.

1.

But the principal thing is this: confirmation is the consummation and perfection, the corroboration and strength of baptism and baptismal grace; for in baptism we undertake to do our duty, but in confirmation we receive strength to do it; in baptism others promise for us, in confirmation we undertake for ourselves, we ease our godfathers and godmothers of their burden, and take it upon our own shoulders, together with the advantage of the prayers of the bishop and all the church made then on our behalf; in baptism we give up our names to Christ, but in confirmation we put our seal to the profession, and God puts His seal to the promise. It is very remarkable what S. Paul says of the beginnings of our being Christians, ὁ τῆς ἀρχῆς τοῦ Χριστοῦ λόγος, 'the word of the beginning of Christ;' Christ begins with us, He gives us His word and admits us, and we by others' hands are brought in; τύπος διδαχῆς εἰς ὃν παρεδόθητε,[10] it is 'the form of doctrine unto which ye were delivered.' Cajetan observes right, that this is a new and emphatical way of

---

[9] [John vii. 38.]
[10] [Rom. vi. 17.]

speaking: we are wholly immerged in our fundamentals; other things are delivered to us, but we are delivered up unto these. This is done in baptism and catechism; and what was the event of it? "Being then made free from sin, ye became the servants of righteousness."[11] Your baptism was for the remission of sins there, and then ye were made free from that bondage; and what then? why then in the next place, when ye came to consummate this procedure, when the baptized was confirmed, then he became a servant of righteousness, that is, then the Holy Ghost descended upon you, and enabled you to walk in the Spirit; then the seed of God was first thrown into your hearts by a celestial influence. *Spiritus sanctus in baptisterio plenitudinem tribuit ad innocentiam, sed in confirmation augmentum præstat ad gratiam*, said Eusebius Emissenus:[12] in baptism we are made innocent, in confirmation we receive the increase of the Spirit of grace; in that we are regenerated unto life, in this we are strengthened unto battle. *Dono sapientiæ illuminamur, ædificamur, erudimur, instruimur, confirmamur,*[13] *ut illam sancti Spiritus vocem audire possimus, Intellectum tibi dabo, et instruam te in hac via qua gradieris*, said P. Melchiades,[14] "we are enlightened by the gift of wisdom, we are built up, taught, instructed and confirmed, so that we may hear that voice of the Holy Spirit, 'I will give unto thee an understanding heart, and teach thee in the way wherein thou shalt walk:'" For so,

> Signari populos effuso pignore sancto,
> Mirandæ virtutis opus,—[15]

'it is a work of great and wonderful power when the holy pledge of God is poured forth upon the people.' This is that power from on high which first descended in Pentecost, and afterward was

---

[11] [ver. 18.]
[12] Serm. de Pentecoste. [The words are from Melchiades, ad episc. Hispan. c. 2.—Hallier (p. 69) quotes them from 'Eusebius Emiss. seu auctor ser. de Pentecoste.']
[13] [leg. 'consummamur.']
[14] [ut in not. 12, supra.]—Habetur apud Gratian. de consecrate. dist. 5. c. 'Spiritus S.' [The chapter in Gratian contains the preceding passage from Melchiades, but not this.]
[15] Tertul. advers. Marcion., lib. i. car. c. 3. [p. 630.]

ministered by prayer and imposition of the apostolical and episcopal hands, and comes after the other gift of remission of sins. *Vides quod non simpliciter hoc fit, sed multa opus est virtute ut detur Spiritus sanctus, non enim idem est assequi remissionem peccatorum et accipere virtutem illam*, said S. Chrysostom;[16] 'you see that this is not easily done, but there is need of much power from on high to give the Holy Spirit, for it is not all one to obtain remission of sins and to have received this virtue or power from above.' *Quamvis enim continuo transituris sufficiant regenerationis beneficia, victuris tamen necessaria sunt confirmationis auxilia*, said Melchiades;[17] 'although to them that die presently the benefits of regeneration (baptismal) are sufficient, yet to them that live the auxiliaries of confirmation are necessary.' For according to the saying of S. Leo[18] in his epistle to Nicetas the bishop of Aquileia, commanding that heretics returning to the church should be confirmed with invocation of the Holy Spirit and imposition of hands, 'they have only received the form of baptism *sine sanctificationis virtute*, without the virtue of sanctification;' meaning that this is the proper effect of confirmation. For in short, "although the newly-listed soldiers in human warfare are enrolled in the number of them that are to fight, yet they are not brought to battle till they be more trained and exercised: so although by baptism every one is ascribed into the catalogue of believers, yet he receives more strength and grace for the sustaining and overcoming the temptations of the flesh, the world, and the devil, only by imposition of the bishop's hands." They are words which I borrowed from a late synod at Rhemes.[19] That's the first remark of blessing; in confirmation we receive strength to do all that which was for us undertaken in baptism: for the apostles themselves (as the holy fathers observe) were timorous in the faith until they were confirmed in Pentecost, but after the reception of the Holy Ghost they waxed valiant in the faith and in all their spiritual combats.

---

[16] Hom. xviii. in Act. [tom. ix. p. 147.]
[17] [ut in not. 12, supra.]
[18] [ep. lxxix. cap. 7. p. 148.]
[19] [Bochell. decret. Eccles. Gall., lib. ii. tit. 5. cap. 11.]

2.

In confirmation we receive the Holy Ghost as the earnest of our inheritance, as the seal of our salvation: καλοῦμεν σφραγῖδα, ὡς συντήρησιν καὶ τῆς δεσποτείας σημείωσιν, saith Gregory Nazianzen;[20] 'we therefore call it a seal or signature, as being a guard and custody to us, and a sign of the Lord's dominion over us.' The confirmed person is πρόβατον ἐσφραγισμένον, 'a sheep that is marked,' which thieves do not so easily steal and carry away. To the same purpose are those words of Theodoret,[21] Ἀνάμνησον σαυτὸν τῆς ἱερᾶς μυσταγωγίας, ἐν ᾗ οἱ τελούμενοι, μετὰ τὴν ἄρνησιν τοῦ τυράννου, καὶ τὴν τοῦ Βασιλέως ὁμολογίαν, οἱονεὶ σφραγῖδά τινα βασιλικὴν δέχονται τοῦ πνευματικοῦ μύρου τὸ χρίσμα, ὡς ἐν τύπῳ τῷ μύρῳ τὴν ἀόρατον τοῦ παναγίου Πνεύματος χάριν ὑποδεχόμενοι· 'remember that holy mystagogy, in which they who were initiated, after the renouncing that tyrant (the devil and all his works) and the confession of the true king (Jesus Christ), have received the chrism of spiritual unction like a royal signature, by that unction, as in a shadow, perceiving the invisible grace of the most Holy Spirit.' That is, in confirmation we are sealed for the service of God and unto the day of redemption; then it is that the seal of God is had by us, "The Lord knoweth who are His." *Quomodo vero dices, Dei sum, si notas non produxeris?* said S. Basil,[22] "How can any man say I am God's sheep unless he produce the marks?' *Signati estis Spiritu promissionis per sanctissimum divinum Spiritum, Domini grex effecti sumus,* said Theophylact.[23] 'When we are thus sealed by the most holy and divine Spirit of promise, then we are truly of the Lord's flock, and marked with His seal;' that is, when we are rightly confirmed, then He descends into our souls; and though He does not operate (it may be) presently, but as the reasonable soul works in its due time and by the order of nature, by opportunities and new fermentations and actualities; so does the Spirit of God; when He is brought into use, when He is prayed for with love and assiduity, when He is caressed tenderly, when He is used lovingly, when we

---

[20] [Orat. xl. cap. 4. tom. i. p. 693 B.]
[21] Comment. in Cantic., c. i. 2. [tom. ii. part. 1. p. 30.]
[22] In adhort. ad baptis. [tom. ii. p. 117 B.]
[23] [leg. 'Theodoret.' in Eph. i. 13.]

obey His motions readily, when we delight in His words greatly, then we find it true that the soul had a new life put into her, a principle of perpetual actions: but the 'tree planted by the water's side' does not presently bear fruit, but in its due season. By this Spirit we are then sealed; that whereas God hath laid up an inheritance for us in the kingdom of heaven, and in the faith of that we must live and labour, to confirm this faith God hath given us this pledge, the Spirit of God is a witness to us, and tells us by His holy comforts, by the peace of God and the quietness and refreshments of a good conscience, that God is our Father, that we are His sons and daughters, and shall be co-heirs with Jesus in His eternal kingdom. In baptism we are made the sons of God, but we receive the witness and testimony of it in confirmation. This is ὁ παράκλητος, the Holy Ghost the Comforter, this is He whom Christ promised and did send in Pentecost, and was afterwards ministered and conveyed by prayer and imposition of hands: and by this Spirit He makes the confessors bold and the martyrs valiant, and the tempted strong, and the virgins to persevere, and widows to sing His praises and His glories. And this is that excellency which the church of God called the Lord's seal, and teaches to be imprinted in confirmation; τὸ τέλειον φυλακτήριον, τὴν σφραγῖδα τοῦ Κυρίου, 'a perfect phylactery or guard, even the Lord's seal,' so Eusebius[24] calls it.

I will not be so curious as to enter into a discourse of the philosophy of this, but I shall say that they who are curious in the secrets of nature, and observe external signatures in stones, plants, fruits and shells, of which naturalists make many observations and observe strange effects, and the more internal signatures in minerals and living bodies of which chymists discourse strange secrets, may easily, if they please, consider that it is infinitely credible that in higher essences, even in spirits, there may be signatures proportionable, wrought more immediately and to greater purposes by a divine hand. I only point at this, and so pass it over, as (it may be) not fit for every man's consideration.

---

[24] [leg. 'Clem. Alex.'] apud Euseb. [hist. Eccles., iii. 23.]

And now if any man shall say, "We see no such things as you talk of, and find the confirmed people the same after as before, no better and no wiser, not richer in gifts, not more adorned with graces, nothing more zealous for Christ's kingdom, not more comforted with hope, or established by faith, or built up with charity; they neither speak better nor live better;" what then, does it therefore follow that the Holy Ghost is not given in confirmation? Nothing less: for is not Christ given us in the sacrament of the Lord's supper? do not we receive His body and His blood? are we not made all one with Christ, and He with us? And yet it is too true, that when we arise from that holy feast, thousands there are that find no change.—But there are in this two things to be considered;—

One is, that the changes which are wrought upon our souls are not after the manner of nature, visible and sensible, and with observation. "The kingdom of God cometh not with observation:" for it is within you, and is only discerned spiritually, and produces its effects by the method of heaven, and is first apprehended by faith, and is endeared by charity, and at last is understood by holy and kind experiences. And in this there is no more objection against confirmation than against baptism, or the Lord's supper, or any other ministry evangelical.

The other thing is this: if we do not find the effects of the Spirit in confirmation it is our faults. For He is received by moral instruments, and is intended only as a help to our endeavours, to our labours and our prayers, to our contentions and our mortifications, to our faith and to our hope, to our patience and to our charity. *Non adjuvari dicitur qui nihil facit,* 'he that does nothing cannot be said to be helped.' Unless we in these instances do our part of the work, it will be no wonder if we lose His part of the co-operation and supervening blessing. He that comes under the bishop's hands to receive the gift of the Holy Ghost, will come with holy desires and a longing soul, with an open hand and a prepared heart; he will purify the house of the Spirit for the entertainment of so divine a guest; he will receive Him with humility, and follow Him with obedience, and delight Him with purities: and he that does thus, let him make the objection if he can, and tell me,—Does he say that Jesus is the Lord? He cannot say this but by the Holy Ghost. Does he love his brother? If he does, then the Spirit of God abides in him. Is Jesus Christ formed in him? does He live by the laws of the Spirit? does he obey His commands? does he attend His motions? hath he no earnest desires to serve God? If he have not, then in vain hath he received either baptism or confirmation: but if he have, it is certain that of himself he cannot do these things; he cannot of himself think a good thought. Does he therefore think well? That is from the Holy Spirit of God.

To conclude this enquiry. "The Holy Ghost is promised to all men to profit withal;"[25] that's plain in scripture. Confirmation, or prayer and imposition of the bishop's hand, is the solemnity and rite used in scripture for the conveying of that promise, and the effect is felt in all the sanctifications and changes of the soul; and he that denies these things hath not faith, nor the true notices of religion, or the spirit of christianity. Hear what the scriptures yet further say in this mystery. "Now He which confirmeth or stablisheth us with you in Christ, and hath anointed us, is God; who hath also sealed us, and given the earnest of the Spirit in our hearts."[26] Here is a description of the whole mysterious part of this rite. God is the author of the grace: the apostles and all Christians are the suscipients, and receive this grace: by this grace we are adopted and incorporated into Christ; God hath anointed us; that is, He hath given us this unction from above, He hath 'sealed us by His spirit,' made us His own, bored our ears through, made us free by His perpetual service, and hath done all these things in token of a greater; He hath given us His spirit to testify to us that He will give us of His glory. These words of S. Paul, besides that they evidently contain in them the spiritual part of this ritual, are also expounded of the rite and sacramental itself by S. Chrysostom, Theodoret and Theophylact, that I may name no more. For in this mystery *Christos nos efficit, et misericordiam Dei nobis annunciat per Spiritum sanctum,* said S. John Damascene,[27] 'He makes us His anointed ones, and by the Holy Spirit He declares His eternal mercy

---

[25] [1 Cor. xii. 7.]
[26] [2 Corn. i. 21, 22.]
[27] Lib. iv. De fide, c. 10. [al. 9. tom. i. p. 262.]

towards us.' *Nolite tangere christos meos*, 'Touch not Mine anointed ones.' For when we have this signature of the Lord upon us the devils cannot come near to hurt us, unless we consent to their temptations and drive the Holy Spirit of the Lord from us.

Chapter Seven
Of preparation to confirmation, and the circumstances of receiving it.

If confirmation have such gracious effects, why do we confirm little children, whom in all reason we cannot suppose to be capable and receptive of such graces? It will be no answer to this if we say, that this very question is asked concerning the baptism of infants, to which as great effects are consequent, even pardon of all our sins and the new birth and regeneration of the soul unto Christ; for in these things the soul is wholly passive, and nothing is required of the suscipient but that he put in no bar against the grace, which because infants cannot do, they are capable of baptism: but it follows not that therefore they are capable of confirmation, because this does suppose them such as to need new assistances, and is a new profession, and a personal undertaking, and therefore requires personal abilities, and cannot be done by others, as in the case of baptism. The aids given in confirmation are in order to our contention and our danger, our temptation and spiritual warfare; and therefore it will not seem equally reasonable to confirm children as to baptize them.

To this I answer, that in the primitive church confirmation was usually administered at the same time with baptism; for we find many records that when the office of baptism was finished and the baptized person divested of the white robe, the person was carried again to the bishop to be confirmed, as I have already shewn out of Dionysius[1]

---

[1] Cap. iv. part. 3. De eccles. hier.—Melchiad. epist. ad episc. Hispan.—Orde Rom. cap. De die sabbati S. Pasch.—Alcuin. De divin. office., c. 19

and divers others. The reasons why anciently they were ministered immediately after one another is, not only because the most of them that were baptized were of years to choose their religion, and did so, and therefore were capable of all that could be consequent to baptism, or annexed to it, or ministered with it, and therefore were also at the same time communicated as well as confirmed; but also because the solemn baptisms were at solemn times of the year, at Easter only and Whitsuntide, and only in the cathedral or bishop's church in the chief city, whither when the catechumens came, and had the opportunity of the bishop's presence, they took the advantage *ut sacramento utroque renascantur*, as S. Cyprian's[2] expression is, that they might be regenerated by both the mysteries, and they also had the third added, viz., the holy eucharist.

This simultaneous ministration hath occasioned some few of late to mistake confirmation for a part of baptism, but no distinct rite, or of distinct effect, save only that it gave ornament and complement or perfection to the other. But this is infinitely confuted by the very first ministry of confirmation in the world: for there was a great interval between S. Philip's baptizing and the apostle's confirming the Samaritans; where also the difference is made wider by the distinction of the minister; a deacon did one, none but an apostle and his successor a bishop could do the other: and this being of so universal a practice and doctrine in the primitive church, it is a great wonder that any learned men could suffer an error in so apparent a case. It is also clear in two other great remarks of the practice of the primitive church: the one is of them who were baptized in their sickness, the οἱ ἐν νόσῳ παραλαμβάνοντες, καὶ εἶτα ἀναστάντες, when they recovered they were commanded to address themselves to the bishop to be confirmed; which appears in the thirty-eighth canon of the council of Eliberis, and the forty-sixth canon of the council of Laodicea, which I have before cited upon other occasions: the other is that of heretics returning to the church, who were confirmed not only long after baptism, but after their apostasy and their conversion.

---

[2] [vid. Chap. 1, not. 22, supra.]

For although episcopal confirmation was the enlargement of baptismal grace, and commonly administered the same day, yet it was done by interposition of distinct ceremonies, and not immediately in time. Honorius Augustodunensis[3] tells, that when the baptized on the eighth day had laid aside their mitres or proper habit used in baptism, then they were usually confirmed or consigned with chrism in the forehead by the bishop. And when children were baptized irregularly or besides the ordinary way in villages and places distant from the bishop, confirmation was deferred, said Durandus. And it is certain that this affair did not last long without variety: sometimes they ministered both together; sometimes at greater, sometimes at lesser distances; and it was left indifferent in the church to do the one or the other, or the third, according to the opportunity and the discretion of the bishop.

But afterward in the middle and descending ages it grew to be a question, not whether it were lawful or not, but which were better, to confirm infants or to stay to their childhood or to their riper years. Aquinas,[4] Bonaventure[5] and some others say it is best that they be confirmed in their infancy, *quia dolus non est, nec obicem ponunt,* they are then without craft, and cannot hinder the descent of the Holy Ghost upon them. And indeed it is most agreeable with the primitive practice, that if they were baptized in infancy they should then also be confirmed; according to that of the famous epistle of Melchiades to the bishops of Spain,[6] *Ita conjuncta sunt hæc duo sacramenta, ut ab invicem, nisi morte præveniente, non possint separari, et unum sine altero rite perfici non potest.* Where although he expressly affirms the rites to be two, yet unless it be in cases of necessity they are not to be severed, and one without the other is not perfect; which in the sense formerly mentioned is true, and so to be understood, that "to him who is baptized and is not confirmed something very considerable is wanting, and therefore they ought to be joined, though not immediately, yet εὐχρόνως, according to reason able occasions and

---

[3] Vide Cassandrum, Schol. ad hymn. eccl. [p. 218.—opp. fol. Par. 1616.]
[4] [3 sum. q. lxxii. art. 8.]
[5] [In lib. iv. dist. 7. art. 3. qu. tom. v. part. 2., p. 97.]
[6] [cap. 2. p. 698.]

accidental causes." But in this there must needs be a liberty in the church, not only for the former reasons, but also because the apostles themselves were not confirmed till after they had received the sacrament of the Lord's supper.

Others therefore say that to confirm them of riper years is with more edification. The confession of faith is more voluntary, the election is wiser, the submission to Christ's discipline is more acceptable, and they have more need, and can make better use of their strengths then derived by the Holy Spirit of God upon them: and to this purpose it is commanded in the canon law that they who are confirmed should be *perfectæ ætatis*, 'of full age;' upon which the gloss[7] says, *Perfectum vocat forte duodecim annorum*, 'twelve years old was a full age, because at those years they might then be admitted to the lower services in the church.' But the reason intimated and implied by the canon is because of the preparation to it; "they must come fasting, and they must make public confession of their faith." And indeed that they should do so is matter of great edification, as also are the advantages of choice and other preparatory abilities and dispositions above mentioned. They are matter of edification, I say, when they are done; but then the delaying of them so long before they be done, and the wanting the aids of the Holy Ghost conveyed in that ministry, are very prejudicial, and are not matter of edification.

But therefore there is a third way, which the church of England and Ireland follows, and that is, that after infancy, but yet before they understand too much of sin, and when they can competently understand the fundamentals of religion, then it is good to bring them to be confirmed, that the Spirit of God may prevent their youthful sins, and Christ by His word and by His Spirit may enter and take possession at the same time. And thus it was in the church of England long since provided and commanded by the laws of king Edgar [A.D. 967], cap. 15,[8] *ut nullus ab episcopo confirmari diu nimium detrectarit*, 'that none should too long put off his being confirmed by the bishop;' that is, as is best expounded by the perpetual practice almost ever since,

---

[7] De consecrate. dist. v. c. 'Ut jejuni.' [sc. c. vi. col. 2224.]
[8] [Wilkins, Concil., tom. i. p. 226.]

as soon as ever by catechism and competent instruction they were prepared, it should not be deferred. If it have been omitted (as of late years it hath been too much) as we do in baptism, so in this also, it may be taken at any age, even after they have received the Lord's supper; as I observed before in the practice and example of the apostles themselves, which in this is an abundant warrant; but still the sooner the better. I mean after that reason begins to dawn; but ever it must be taken care of that the parents and godfathers, the ministers and masters, see that the children be catechized and well instructed in the fundamentals of their religion.

For this is the necessary preparation to the most advantageous reception of this holy ministry. *In ecclesiis potissimum Latinis non nisi adultiore ætate pueros admitti videmus, vel hanc certe ob causam, ut parentibus, susceptoribus et ecclesiarum præfectis, occasio detur pueros de fide, quam in baptismo professi sunt, diligentius instituendi et admonendi*, said the excellent Cassander;[9] 'in the Latin churches they admit children of some ripeness of age, that they may be more diligently taught and instructed in the faith.' And to this sense agree S. Austin,[10] Walafridus Strabo,[11] Ruardus Lovaniensis,[12] and Mr. Calvin.[13]

For this was ever the practice of the primitive church, to be infinitely careful of catechizing those who came and desired to be admitted to this holy rite; they used exorcisms or catechisms to prepare them to baptism and confirmation. I said 'exorcisms or catechisms,' for they were the same thing; if the notion be new, yet I the more willingly declare it, not only to free the primitive church from the suspicion of superstition in using charms or exorcisms (according to the modern sense of the word) or casting of the devil out of innocent children, but also to remonstrate the perpetual practice of catechizing children in the eldest and best times of the church. Thus the greek scholiast upon Harmenopulus[14] renders the

---

[9] Consultationis, cap. 9. [p. 936 fol. Par. 1616.]
[10] Serm. cxvi. In ramis palmarum. [al. serm. cclxvii. tom. v. append. col. 441.]
[11] De reb. ecclesiast., c. 26. [p.964.]
[12] [De confirm. sc. in artic. xii.—opp. fol. Col. Agr. 1582. tom. ii. p. 140 sqq.]
[13] [See Cassander, as above, note 9.]
[14] [Epit. s. canon. sect. i. tit. 9. Apud Leunclav. Jus Græcorum, p. 16.]

word ἐφορκιστὰς by κατηχητὰς, the primitive exorcist was the catechist; and Balsamon[15] upon the twenty-sixth canon of the council of Laodicea says that to exorcize is nothing but to catechize the unbelievers; Τινὲς ἐπεχείρουν ἐφορκίζειν, τουτέστι κατηχεῖν ἀπίστους, 'some undertook to exorcize, that is,' says he, 'to catechize the unbelievers:' and S. Cyril, in his preface to his catechisms,[16] speaking to the *Illuminati, Festinent,* says he, *pedes tui ad catecheses audiendas, exorcismos studiose suscipe, &c.,* 'let your feet run hastily to hear the catechisms, studiously receive the exorcisms, although thou beest already inspired and exorcized;' that is, although you have been already instructed in the mysteries, yet still proceed; 'for without exorcisms' or catechisms 'the soul cannot go forward, since they are divine and gathered out of the scriptures.' And the reason why these were called exorcisms he adds, 'because when the exorcists or catechists by the Spirit of God produce fear in your hearts, and do enkindle the Spirit as in a furnace, the devil flies away, and salvation and hope of life eternal does succeed:' according to that of the evangelist[17] concerning Christ, "they were astonished at His doctrine, for His word was with power;" and that of S. Luke concerning Paul and Barnabas, "the deputy, when he saw what was done, was astonished at the doctrine of the Lord;"[18] it is the Lord's doctrine that hath the power to cast out devils and work miracles; catechisms are the best exorcisms: "let us therefore, brethren, abide in hope, and persevere in catechizings," saith S. Cyril, "although they be long, and produced with many words or discourses."[19] The same also we find in S. Gregory Nazianzen,[20] and S. Austin.[21]

The use that I make of this notion is principally to be an exhortation to all of the clergy, that they take great care to catechize all their people, to bring up children in the nurture and admonition

---

[15] [Bevereg. Synod., tom. i. p. 464.]
[16] [cap. ix. p. 7.]
[17] [Luke iv. 32.]
[18] [Acts xiii. 12.]
[19] [ubi supra, p. 8.]
[20] Orat. de bapt. [orat. xl. cap. 27. tom. i. p. 712 E.]
[21] In psalm. lxviii. [? lxv. § 17. tom. iv. col. 651.]

of the Lord, to prepare a holy seed for the service of God, to cultivate the young plants and to dress the old ones, to take care that those who are men in the world be not mere babes and uninstructed in Christ, and that they who are children in age may be wise unto salvation: for by this means we shall rescue them from early temptations, when being so prepared they are so assisted by a divine ministry; we shall weaken the devil's power, by which he too often and too much prevails upon uninstructed and unconfirmed youth. For μύρον βεβαίωσις τῆς ὁμολογίας, 'confirmation is the firmament of our profession;' but we profess nothing till we be catechized. Catechizings are our best preachings, and by them we shall give the best accounts of our charges, while in behalf of Christ we make disciples, and take prepossession of infant understandings, and by this holy rite, by prayer and imposition of hands, we minister the Holy Spirit to them, and so prevent and disable the artifices of the devil; "for we are not ignorant of his devices," how he enters as soon as he can, and taking advantage of their ignorance and their passion, seats himself so strongly in their hearts and heads.

Turpius ejicitur quam non admittitur hostis,[22]

It is harder to cast the devil out than to keep him out. Hence it is that the youth are so corrupted in their manners, so devilish in their natures, so cursed[23] in their conversation, so disobedient to parents, so wholly given to vanity and idleness; they learn to swear before they can pray, and to lie as soon as they can speak. It is not my sense alone, but was long since observed by Gerson[24] and Gulielmus Parisiensis,[25] *propter cessationem confirmationis tepiditas grandior est in fidelibus, et fidei defensione*; there is a coldness and deadness in religion, and it proceeds from the neglect of confirmation rightly ministered, and after due

---

[22] [Ovid., trist. v. 6. 13.]
[23] [i.e. 'perverse, froward;' see Johnson and Richardson on 'curst,' 'cursed,' and 'accursed'; cf. p. 217, note e, Taylor, *Whole Works*, ed. Heber and Eden, vol. 5.]
[24] De exterminat. schism. [leg. 'De officio prælatorum,' &c. Opp. tom. iv. col. 103.—The reader on referring to the page will see how the mistake in reference arose.]
[25] [Apud Gerson. ubi supra.]

preparations and dispositions. A little thing will fill a child's head; teach them to say their prayers, tell them the stories of the life and death of Christ, cause them to love the holy Jesus with their first love, make them afraid of a sin; let the principles which God hath planted in their very creation, the natural principles of justice and truth, of honesty and thankfulness, of simplicity and obedience, be brought into act and habit, and confirmation by the holy sermons of the gospel. If the guides of souls would have their people holy, let them teach holiness to their children, and then they will, at least, have a new generation unto God, better than this wherein we now live. They who are most zealous in this particular will with most comfort reap the fruit of their labours and the blessings of their ministry; and by the numbers which every curate presents to his bishop fitted for confirmation, he will in proportion render an account of his stewardship with some visible felicity. And let it be remembered, that in the last rubric of the office of confirmation in our liturgy it is made into a law, that "none should be admitted to the holy communion until such time as he could say the catechism and be confirmed;" which was also a law and custom in the primitive church, as appears in S. Dionysius his Ecclesiastical Hierarchy, and the matter of fact is notorious. Among the Helvetians they are forbidden to contract marriages before they are well instructed in the catechism; and in a late synod at Bourges,[26] the curates are commanded to threaten all that are not confirmed, that they shall never receive the Lord's supper, nor be married. And in effect the same is of force in our church; for the married persons being to receive the sacrament at their marriage, and none are to receive but those that are confirmed, the same law obtains with us as with the Helvetians or the Synodus Bituricensis.

There is another little enquiry which I am not willing to omit; but the answer will not be long, because there is not much to be said on either side. Some enquire whether the holy rite of confirmation can be ministered any more than once. S. Austin[27] seems to be of

---

[26] [vid. Chap. 5., not. 13, supra.]
[27] Lib. iii. de Bapt., c. 16. [tom. ix. col. 117.]

opinion that it may be repeated. *Quid enim aliud est impositio manuum nisi oratio super hominem?* Confirmation is a solemn prayer over a man; and if so, why it may not be reiterated can have nothing in the nature of the thing; and the Greeks do it frequently, but they have no warranty from the scripture, nor from any of their own ancient doctors. Indeed when any did return from heresy they confirmed them, as I have proved out of the first and second council of Arles, the council of Laodicea, and the second council of Sevil: but upon a closer intuition of the thing, I find they did so only to such who did not allow of confirmation in their sects, such as the Novatians and the Donatists. *Novatiani pænitentiam a suo conventu arcent penitus, et iis qui ab ipsis tinguntur sacrum chrismia non præbent; quocirca qui ex hac hæresi corpori ecclesiæ conjunguntur benedicti patres ungi jusserunt*: so Theodoret.[28] For that reason only the Novatians were to be confirmed upon their conversion, because they had it not before. I find also they did confirm the converted Arians; but the reason is given in the first council of Arles,[29] *quia propria lege utuntur*, 'they had a way of their own:' that is, as the gloss saith upon the canon *De Arianis, De consecrat. dist.* 4,[30] their baptism was not in the name of the holy Trinity; and so their baptism being null, or at least suspected, to make all as sure as they could, they confirmed them. The same also is the case of the Bonosiaci in the second council of Arles, though they were (as some of the Arians also were) baptized in the name of the most holy Trinity; but it was a suspected matter, and therefore they confirmed them: but to such persons who had been rightly baptized and confirmed they never did repeat it. Πνεύματος ἁγίου σφραγῖδα δώῃ ἀνεξάλειπτον, 'the gift of the Spirit is an indelible seal,' saith S. Cyril;[31] ἀνεπιχείρητον S. Basil[32] calls it, it is 'inviolable.' They who did re-baptize, did also re-confirm. But as it was an error in S. Cyprian and the Africans to do the first, so was the second also, in case they had done it; for I find no mention expressly that they did the latter but upon the fore-mentioned

---

[28] Lib. iii. hæret. fabul. [cap. 5.]
[29] [can. 8. tom. i. col. 265.]
[30] [can. 109. col. 2197.]
[31] Cyril. Hieros. in procatech. [ad fin. p. 14 A.]
[32] [Hom. xiii. tom. ii. p. 117 D.]

accounts, and either upon supposition of the invalidity of their first pretended baptism, or their not using at all of confirmation in their heretical conventicles. But the repetition of confirmation is expressly forbidden[33] by the council of Tarracon, cap. 6, and by P. Gregory the second: and *Sanctum chrisma collatum et altaris honor propter consecrationem (quæ per episcopos tan tum exercenda et conferenda sunt) evelli non queunt,* said the fathers in a council at Toledo,[34] 'Confirmation and holy orders, which are to be given by bishops alone, can never be annulled, and therefore they can never be repeated.' And this relies upon those severe words of S. Paul, having spoken of "the foundation of the doctrine of baptisms and laying on of hands," he says, "if they fall away, they can never be renewed;"[35] that is, the ministry of baptism and confirmation can never be repeated. To Christians that sin after these ministrations there is only left a νήψατε, *expergiscimini,* that they 'arise from slumber,' and stir up the graces of the Holy Ghost. Every man ought to be careful that he 'do not grieve the Holy Spirit;' but if he does, yet let him not quench Him, for that is a desperate case. Φύλαττε τὸν φυλακτικόν· the Holy Spirit is the great conservative of the new life; only 'keep the keeper,' take care that the Spirit of God do not depart from you: for the great ministry of the Spirit is but once; for as baptism is, so is confirmation.

I end this discourse with a plain exhortation out of S. Ambrose[36] upon those words of S. Paul, "He that confirmeth us with you in Christ is God;" *Repete quia accepisti signaculum spirituale, spiritum sapientiæ et intellectus, spiritum consilii atque virtutis, spiritum cognitionis atque pietatis, spiritum sancti timoris, et serva quod accepisti; signavit te Deus Pater, confirmavit te Christus Dominus;* 'Remember that thou, who hast been confirmed, hast received the spiritual signature, the spirit of wisdom and understanding, the spirit of counsel and strength, the spirit of knowledge and godliness, the spirit of holy fear; keep what thou hast received: the Father hath sealed thee, and Christ thy Lord hath

---

[33] Apud Gratian. de consecrate., dist. v. cap. [8.] 'Dictum est,' et cap. [9.] 'De homine.' [col. 2224.]
[34] Concil. Toletan. viii. can. 7. [tom. iii. col 963.]
[35] [Heb. vi. 6.]
[36] [De mystic., cap. vii. fin.]

confirmed thee' by His divine Spirit, and He will never depart from thee, εἰ μὴ δι᾽ ἔργων φαυλότητα ἡμεῖς ἑαυτοὺς ταύτης ἀποξενώσωμεν,[37] 'unless by evil works we estrange Him from us.' The same advice is given by Prudentius,[38]

> Cultor Dei, memento
> Te fontis et lavacri
> Rorem subîsse sanctum,
> Et chrismate innotatum.[39]

Remember how great things ye have received, and what God hath done for you: ye are of His flock and His militia; ye are now to fight His battles, and therefore to put on His armour, and to implore His auxiliaries, and to make use of His strengths, and always to be on His side against all His and all our enemies. But he that desires grace must not despise to make use of all the instruments of grace. For though God communicates His invisible Spirit to you, yet that He is pleased to do it by visible instruments is more than He needs, but not more than we do need. And therefore since God descends to our infirmities, let us carefully and lovingly address ourselves to His ordinances: that as we receive remission of sins by the washing of water, and the body and blood of Christ by the ministry of consecrated symbols; so we may receive the Holy Ghost *sub ducibus christianæ militiæ*, by the prayer and imposition of the bishop's hands, whom our Lord Jesus hath separated to this ministry. "For if you corroborate yourself by baptism" (they are the words of S. Gregory Nazianzen[40]) "and then take heed for the future, by the most excellent and firmest aids consigning your mind and body with the unction from above" (viz . in the holy rite of confirmation) "with the Holy Ghost, as the children of Israel did with the aspersion on the door posts in the night of the death of the first-born of Egypt, what (evil) shall happen to you?" meaning, that no evil can invade you: "and what aid shall you get? if you sit down, you shall be without fear; and if you

---

[37] Zonar. in can Laodicen. 48. [Bevereg. Synod., tom. i. p. 476.]
[38] [Cathemer. hymn. vi. 125. p. 307.]
[39] ['innovatum' edd.]
[40] Orat. in sanctum. lavacrum. [orat. xl. cap. 15. tom. i. p. 701.]

rest, your sleep shall be sweet unto you." But if when ye have received the Holy Spirit you live not according to His divine principles, you will lose Him again; that is, you will lose all the blessing, though the impression does still remain till ye turn quite apostates: *In pessimis hominibus manebit, licet ad judicium*, saith S. Austin;[41] the Holy Ghost will remain, either as a testimony of your unthankfulness unto condemnation, or else as a seal of grace, and an earnest of your inheritance of eternal glory.

---

[41] Lib. ii. contra. lit. Petil., c. 104 [tom ix. col. 293.]

A Note on the Text

A Discourse of Confirmation was originally published in 1663. This edition is a new typesetting of the *Discourse* as it was published in Volume V of *The Whole Works of the Right Rev. Jeremy Taylor*, edited by Reginald Heber, revised by Charles Page Eden, and published in London by Longman, Brown, Green, and Longmans, et al. in 1849. Only slight changes have been made; for instance, the alphabetical footnote system has been replaced with a numeric one. Citations that refer to other parts of the *Discourse* have been changed accordingly. If a footnote made reference to a citation given earlier in Volume V but not within the *Discourse* itself, the footnote in this present edition now references *The Whole Works*. If you believe you have found an error, please email seminarystreetpress@gmail.com so that corrections can be incorporated into a future printing.

The Library of Anglican Theology

No. 1   **Perfective Unction: A Discourse of Confirmation**
Jeremy Taylor

No. 2   **The Incarnation of the Son of God**
Charles Gore

No. 3   **Early Sermons from the African Episcopal Church of St. Thomas, Philadelphia**
Absalom Jones & William Douglass

No. 4   **The Ministry of Consolation: A Guide to Confession** *and* **The Shadow of the Holy Week**
Felicia Skene

Printed in Great Britain
by Amazon